Every Grain of Sand
Canadian Perspectives on Ecology and Environment

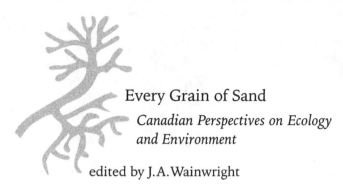

Every Grain of Sand

Canadian Perspectives on Ecology and Environment

edited by J.A. Wainwright

Wilfrid Laurier University Press

We acknowledge the support of the Canada Council for the Arts for our publishing program. We acknowledge the financial support of the Government of Canada through the Book Publishing Industry Development Program for our publishing activities. We acknowledge the Government of Ontario through the Ontario Media Development Corporation's Ontario Book Initiative.

ONTARIO ARTS COUNCIL
CONSEIL DES ARTS DE L'ONTARIO

Library and Archives Canada Cataloguing in Publication

Every grain of sand: Canadian perspectives on ecology and environment / edited by J.A. Wainwright.

Includes bibliographical references.

ISBN 0-88920-453-5

1. Nature—effect of human beings on. 2. Human ecology. 3. Environmental degradation. I. Wainwright, Andy, 1946–

GF75.E94 2004   304.2   C2004-906532-7

© 2004 Wilfrid Laurier University Press
Waterloo, Ontario, Canada
www.wlupress.wlu.ca

Cover design by P.J. Woodland, using photography by Ken Madsen. Text design by P.J. Woodland.

The essay by Monte Hummel is reprinted from *Wintergreen: Reflections from Loon Lake* (Toronto: Key Porter, 1999) with permission of the publisher.

Every reasonable effort has been made to acquire permission for copyright material used in this text, and to acknowledge all such indebtedness accurately. Any errors and omissions called to the publisher's attention will be corrected in future printings.

∞

Printed in Canada

To see a World in a Grain of Sand
And a Heaven in a Wild Flower
Keeps the Human Soul from Care.
—*William Blake*

I am hanging in the balance
of the reality of man.
Like every sparrow falling,
like every grain of sand.
—*Bob Dylan*

Table of Contents

Contents

1

Introduction

J.A. Wainwright

In the first essay of this collection, "The World Is Your Body," Lionel Rubinoff describes the extraordinarily life-affirming bond between humanity and nature "for which humans are phylogenetically disposed [that is, in terms of their evolutionary history], and without which humans are not fully human." In other words, as Rubinoff points out, "there exists an ingrained need and human affinity for nature." This need and affinity have a significant place in the works of all the contributors to this anthology, as critical aspects of people's individual and collective experience on moral, spiritual, and ethical levels.

Unfortunately, there are also human-led forces of destruction and extinction that threaten the well-being of our planet, and it is almost impossible to remain unaware of the increasingly strained relationship between people and the natural world. Media stories report daily on the effects of environmental pollution and other elements of civilization's unchecked "progress" on wildlife species, fish stocks, old-growth forests, safe drinking water, air quality, and even the protective ozone layer that absorbs radiation from the sun's rays as they reach the earth. Today's schoolchildren learn about the steady disappearance of insects, birds, and animals from the world around them; huge draggers scoop fish into oblivion along the Grand Banks and elsewhere; the Amazon rain forest, with its vital system of photosynthesis, is ravaged by mining operations, while British Columbia woodlands are scarred by clear-cutting; Ontario residents become ill or die because groundwater is infected with e-coli bacteria, and families in Cape Breton are apprehensive about long-term exposure to coke oven waste in their neighbourhoods; a giant hole in the sky opens over Antarctica as emissions from household products damage the stratosphere.

Of course, the argument can, and indeed should, be made that those same schoolchildren learn about the setting aside of land for national and provincial parks and wilderness areas; that governments have stepped in to prevent over-fishing and provide forest management; that legal and practical measures are taken to ensure uncontaminated water supplies; and that international agreements have been reached to lower the rate of anti-ozone emissions. But, even given the validity of such arguments, it is clear that not only has the human-natural world relationship become severely impaired, it has also been irrevocably changed by the sheer volume of attacks against living organisms and their habitats. At the very least, as Aldo Leopold suggested over thirty-five years ago, we seem to have outgrown the land.[1] Perhaps worse, as Bill McKibben stressed more recently, we have come to "the end of nature."[2] While this does not mean there is no land left or that the natural world has vanished, it may be that the meaning of our connection to natural processes has been so diminished that we are faced with, according to Rubinoff, "the eclipse ... of a humanity worthy of the human name."

What are some of the fundamental ways to oppose behaviour and policies of injury and extinguishment that stem from what Leanne Simpson calls "greed [and] exploitation," Trish Glazebrook cites as "a patriarchal logic of domination," and Catriona Mortimer-Sandilands describes as the "globalizing commodity fetishism [that] impoverishes nature"; and that result for Anne Marie Dalton in a "radical disjunction between human life and the rest of the natural world" and for Jarmo Jalava in "barbed wire ... stretched between landscapes of divergent human belief"?

One of the most potent forces of opposition to end-of-nature scenarios is positive human memory of the experience of nature. The origins of this anthology lie in my recollections of 1950s boyhood summers spent in the countryside of southern Ontario. For me, at that time, the natural world outside Toronto existed only for unprofaned pleasure that, like the water, trees, and sunlight, would surely go on forever. Without the strength of this retrospection, I would not now be able to consider the ironies of such an anthropocentric view; nor would I have been able to stand with my two young sons on a Black River bridge in Muskoka in the late 1980s, watching the sun's rays open the current's dark sheen below, and cry out my spontaneous pronouncement of thirty-five years before: "It's like a window!"

Karen Krug, in her essay "Growing Roots in Nature," writes of her childhood and youth on a Saskatchewan farm, working with her father in the fields, finding birds' nests or abandoned young rabbits, and developing, unconsciously, a powerful sense of place. For her, decades later, "the farm is still home," and she visits it more often in her mind's eye than in actuality, only now comprehending "the privilege of falling asleep in a silence broken solely by the sounds of night creatures and the elements." Her adult regard for the natural world is first provided by what she learns when she looks back at a self and an environment that have much to teach her. Passing on what she has learned to her daughters, she is convinced that their consideration of the effects of permaculture, resulting from "observing, emulating, and improving upon natural systems" (as opposed to the limited monoculture of her youth), will lead to their comprehension and appreciation of ecological diversities beyond the farm.

Catriona Mortimer-Sandilands, in "The Marginal World," takes her young daughter to the ocean beach of her childhood to show her the transitional spaces or "ecotones ... where cultures, natures, life worlds, experiences, and ideas collide and mingle." Mortimer-Sandilands insists we have a great deal to gain from understanding that we are all marginal creatures and that we should not be afraid of our hybridity or of the biodiversity that helps promote cultural diversity (and vice versa). If we have outgrown the land, then perhaps ecotones, where we have opportunities to engage in dialogue with other species and other disciplinary approaches to nature, can interfere with our power-based constructions of what we deem to be centres and margins. It is clear that Mortimer-Sandilands's memories, with their fertile complexity of what was integral and "pregnant with change," are rich borderland zones between past, present, and possible futures for her daughter.

In her "Reflections of a Zealot," Elizabeth May recalls her childhood as the effective fountainhead of her lifelong activism. The memories of her mother's struggles in the grassroots-based Campaign for Nuclear Disarmament, which contributed in 1963 to the signing by three major superpowers of the Nuclear Test Ban Treaty, prompt her assertion that "from my earliest years, I had no doubt that a single activist can change the world." The deeds of her own teenage years—such as reading Rachel Carson's *Silent Spring*, introducing returnable-bottle legislation in the Connecticut legislature and fighting the spraying of forests with fenitrothion to control the spruce budworm in Cape Breton—are part of a pattern of sustained activism that has led to her present position as executive director of the Sierra Club of Canada. As with Krug and Mortimer-Sandilands, her daughter's possible futures motivate her efforts to convey and employ the remembered lessons of the past.

Our individual pasts are important in the struggle to maintain our humanity, but awareness of our collective cultural history matters just as much if we are to see ourselves as more than isolated beings in the earth's ecosphere. We must read the ironies inherent in Sophocles' *Antigone*, written over two thousand years ago:

> Many the wonders but nothing more wondrous than man.
> ....
> Language and thought like the wind
> and the feelings that make the town
> he has taught himself, and shelter against the cold,
> refuge from rain. He can help himself.
> He faces no future helpless.[3]

As Lionel Rubinoff suggests, humans will indeed face the future helpless if they do not understand their role as stewards and caregivers rather than as masters of the natural world.

Not too long after Sophocles in the ancient world came Christianity. Anne Marie Dalton examines some crucial historical and contemporary connections between religion and ecological crisis in her essay, "Who Cares about the Meadow? The Changing Conversation around Religion and Ecology." Dalton admits that certain interpretations of the Bible have encouraged the crisis, but also points out that various writings in Christian history, including parts of the Bible, provide guidance in regard to environmental issues past and present. It is crucial, for Dalton, that the "radical" be a method employed in programs of social justice leading to simultaneously better treatment of the land and peoples on it; that the integration of scientific and traditional religious accounts of the evolution of the universe be employed for the welfare of earth's entire ecological community; and that there be rejection of essentialist approaches in dealing with the split between humans and the natural world. Only by seeing the small writ large, that is, a meadow as standing for other parts of the earth or for the earth itself, will we be able to move beyond solipsistic conversations and immediate concerns. We may not face the future helpless if we come to understand that "some action in the 1920s to save a small meadow in North Carolina could well have repercussions in the rice paddies of Vietnam" in the early years of the twenty-first century.

Lest we think the ancient Greeks were all of a kind in their approaches to the natural world, Trish Glazebrook, in her "Toward an Ecofeminist Phenomenology of Nature," points out that Aristotle, born only a few decades after Sophocles's death, believed the human relationship with the natural world existed "in a constant state of flux, change, and adaptability" and that "nature ha[d] the first word." The subsequent Christian view, however, had God as the "arch-artisan" of the natural, which ultimately meant the natural was for human benefit, a view supported centuries later with Francis Bacon's "new science," Isaac Newton's "ideology of immutability," and the rigid patriarchal thought and action that drive so much of modern science and technology. In contrast, Goethe recognized that human truths were "provisional, and always open to revision," something Glazebrook supports in her positing of a feminist "erotics of nature." Such erotics connect individual love of nature to larger social and cultural activity and to a sustainable technology based on an alternative science and "eco-logic" that respect nature's purposive process. For Glazebrook, as for Krug, Sandilands, and May, her child's positive interaction with things natural is life-affirming and of vital importance.

In his essay "Romantic Origins of Environmentalism: Wordsworth and Shelley," Onno Oerlemans provides a "green" reading of William Wordsworth's poem "Lines: Written a Few Miles Above Tintern Abbey" to emphasize the Romantic version of phylogenetics that we are "more perceptive, imaginative, and moral" as a result of intimate contact with the natural world. Deep ecological response to this human-nature relationship is not a twentieth-century phenomenon, but one that was alive and well in the last decade of the eighteenth century, and that contained recognition of the natural environment "not as objective and 'other' than our consciousness, but as itself inter-subjective," an idea present in a variety of ways in essays by Leanne Simpson and Monte Hummel.

Hummel, in his Afterword from *Wintergreen: Reflections from Loon Lake*, describes how, near his cabin by the lake, he munches on the same wintergreen berries that small and larger birds and animals ingest: "The beautiful small wintergreen (itself made up of tissues, cells, molecules, atoms, protons, neutrons, quarks, electrons, neutrinos, and leptons) can exist only because it is nested in, and nourished by, an expanding series of interacting ecological envelopes which quite literally give it [and us] life." These envelopes are dependent on a healthy ecosphere, which humans can nurture through, among other things, understanding William Blake's poetic adage on finding worlds and heavens in wildflowers and grains of sand.

But, as Oerlemans also emphasizes, Shelley in "Mount Blanc" presents us with a challenge and a warning. In this poem, nature and consciousness are not one and the same, and humans have no access to the "deep history of the earth." The mountain has its own articulations that we cannot presume to comprehend, and what we are left with is "an awful doubt" about our assumed primary place in the chain of being, even if we are indeed part of the chain and have good intentions in regard to the natural world. This suggests a profound need to reassess our interaction with that world. Instead of being able to meet with nature in transitional spaces, as Sandilands advocates, we may merely be creatures in transition ourselves and alone in the process. The "radical" quality of Shelley's romantic view is its "anti-anthropocentric" basis.

As a Native Canadian, Leanne Simpson might take issue with Dalton's views of the progressive features of Christianity, given her focus in "Listening to Our Ancestors: Rebuilding Indigenous Nations in the Face of Environmental Destruction" on the role of Christian values in the colonization of North American indigenous peoples and environments. But we should compare Edna Manitowabi's words in Simpson's essay, "And when I saw a crane or bulldozer digging into the Earth, it was like a form of rape," to Dalton's quoting of Christian theologian Rosemary Radford Ruether, "Through the raped bodies the earth is raped." Neither is Simpson so far removed from Wordsworth when she emphasizes that "Indigenous world views or philosophical traditions view humans as not only part of the environment or the complex web of life, but as the environment itself." She provides specific illustrations of the assault of clear-cutting and other ways of denigrating or even destroying landscapes and bodies of water, some of which were and are sacred Native sites. Her use of the term "monoculture" to describe the simplistic and damaging efforts to replace what has been lost recalls Karen Krug's criticism of the same practice, and, in their different ways, they present a joint plea for the replacement of a colonial relationship with the land by a more complex, diverse, and self-sustaining system of growth and harvesting.

Ehor Boyanowsky, in "Cutting a Deal with Attila: Confrontation, Capitulation, and Resolution in Environmental Conflict," also underlines particular damage done by logging operations and by pulp mill and mining companies, especially in the form of siltation and pollution of rivers where his cherished steelhead spawn. It is important to oppose visibly such harmful practices and, like Elizabeth May, Boyanowksy underscores the impact of initial environmental endeavours on subsequent activism, placing the origins of the world-famous Greenpeace organization in the philosophy and actions of the three-member Don't Make a Wave Committee in early 1970s British Columbia, and the roots of the Steelhead Society of British Columbia in the previously formed British Columbia Wildlife Federation. Perhaps Boyanowsky's most startling and memorable point is that we must talk to the "enemy" in our environmental wars. Thus, he accentuates the role of British farmers in protecting rather than exterminating foxes *when the hunt is allowed*; he cites the conservation award from the Steelhead Society of British Columbia to logging giant Macmillan Bloedel when it ceased to log old-growth forest and halted clear-cutting on steep slopes; and he stresses "so long as there are predators, there are those who care desperately about their prey."

If we are to understand and communicate our different views on environmental issues, we must acknowledge, as Peter Armitage insists in his essay, "Romancing Labrador: The Social Construction of Wilderness and the Labrador Frontier," that "public opinion is never a tabula rasa when it comes to undertaking advocacy work." We must become aware of the political and cultural origins of the multiple discourses that, for example in Labrador, have shaped human response to natural place. Armitage discusses the historical roles of the imagined and romanticized hinterlands of nineteenth-century Labrador and subsequent wasteland perceptions of wilderness that contributed to the industrialization of what many perceived to be a twentieth-century "resource Eldorado." He also emphasizes the recent emergence of voices "native to Labrador, be they Innu, Inuit, Settler (Metis), or landed immigrants," into debates about industrial vision versus environmental degradation, stressing especially their interference with simplistice divisions along lines of race and class. The abuse of power and the empowerment of those previously marginalized in relation to decisions about land and water use in Labrador need to be addressed through creative contemporary dialogue.

Talking with the "enemy" is something Jarmo Jalava does in his lyrical personal essay, "Prey." As he and his family spend time at two different Ontario cottages, seeking the "quiet space between thoughts where animals dwell and meditators go" (very much an ecotone territory), they meet the human hunters whose trigger-pulling is "ingrained in rural culture" and the all-terrain vehicle riders who recklessly intrude "into the wild anonymity of evolution." Although Jalava, like Krug, Mortimer-Sandilands, and Glazebrook, puts the innocence of his child against experienced purveyors of destruction, and says that an appropriate rite of passage "would be … six months of wilderness solitude, but not during hunting season," he is not prepared to damn completely the armed man who shoots grouse on his rented property. Indeed, in a remarkable, final metaphoric passage that closes this collection, he both appropriates human hunting consciousness and becomes one with natural-world integrity in necessary life-and-death situations.

Simply put, these essays indicate that the better we can understand and help to sustain the familiar ground at our feet or, perhaps more properly, at whose foot we reside, the better we will be able to comprehend and sustain the exchange between ourselves and our earthly neighbours, human and non-human, whose healthy, natural world habitats so contribute to the well-being of our own. As Trish Glazebrook writes, even "rocks talk." We need to listen.

The politics of this anthology, then, are based on our ability to pay heed, appreciate, and act with empathy and wisdom. The essentially (but not essentialist) activist positions taken in Rubinoff's, Dalton's, and Oerlemans's learned treatises support Simpson's, Boyanowsky's, and Armitage's specifically grounded and inclusive advocacy of productive exchange between interest groups with different cultural and political platforms. While some readers might question the efficacy of aesthetic reflection in personal essays—such as those of Krug, Mortimer-Sandilands, and Hummel—in comparison to more direct political expression, such questioning should not last long. These latter writers, as well as Trish Glazebrook, Jarmo Jalava, and myself, through the individual's stories they tell, reveal an outlook and practice of balanced involvement with natural-world issues that responds to the equilibrium inherent in untrammelled natural surroundings and in the best of human relations with them. Even Elizabeth May, who refers to herself as a "zealot," writes moderately and effectively, rather than in strident and aggressive tones, about issues to do with the wholeness of our physical environment and the survival of living creatures, including humankind. I suspect all the contributors to this collection would agree with Aldo Leopold's *A Sand County Almanac* statement that "A thing is right when it tends to preserve the integrity, stability, and beauty of the biotic community. It is wrong when it tends otherwise."[4]

In comparison to a number of American collections on ecology and environment that are readily available, these thirteen essays are meant, from *Canadian* matrices, to engage all readers in respectful dialogue about issues that really know no national borders. They are also meant to encourage conversations with the planet itself. Canadians might say that the "northern" experience, with its specific seasons, growth, and wildlife, is a fundamental part of their national identity, but even if this is so, such human connection to the natural world is part of a much larger process that involves all peoples, whatever their home climate and topography. Besides, climates and topographies differ greatly *within* Canada, and, to their credit, most Canadians prefer to talk about and share their strong sense of local place rather than construct it in any chauvinistic, bordered fashion.

Nine of the contributors to this volume are faculty in programs in environmental studies, philosophy, literature, religion, and criminology at Canadian universities; two are front line activists for the Sierra Club and World Wildlife Fund of Canada; and two are private researchers and consultants in Ontario and Labrador–Newfoundland. All share a fundamental concern about the damaged relationship between humans and the natural world, Garrett Hardin's "'tragedy of the commons,' the condition in which the material demands of the consumptive lifestyle of our political economy far exceed the carrying capacity of the biosphere."[5] All affirm that there is still much to appreciate in, and learn from, this relationship's intricacies and saving graces, and believe it is not yet too late to heal the deep wounds that, left untended, will condemn us to live amidst the depletions of Bill McKibben's "post-natural world."[6] They do not despair, but view humans as involved in a profound cultural and spiritual crisis arising from our flawed exchange with land, water, and life forms to which we are genetically disposed, but with which, historically and culturally, we have been so much in conflict. We must not dream of some lost Eden, but find a way on to harmony with ecosystems as small as the cosmos and as large as a meadow. As Monte Hummel asserts, "We are likely the last generation to have any choice in the matter."

Notes

1 Aldo Leopold, *A Sand County Almanac* (New York: Oxford University Press, 1968), 239.
2 Bill McKibben, "The End of Nature," *The New Yorker*, September 1979, and *The End of Nature* (New York: Random House, 1989). It is fair to point out that Carolyn Merchant published *The Death of Nature: Women, Ecology, and the Scientific Revolution* in 1980.
3 Sophocles, *Antigone*, trans. Elizabeth Wycoff. Cited in Rubinoff, "The World Is Your Body."
4 Leopold, 240.
5 Garrett Hardin, "The Tragedy of the Commons," *Science* 162 (1968). Cited in Rubinoff.
6 It should be noted that Rebecca Solnit, in her *Savage Dreams: A Journey into the Hidden Wars of the American West* (San Francisco: Sierra Club Books, 1994) argues that McKibben's nature is one that never included people in the first place. So, for Solnit, his "post-natural world" marks the end of supposedly pure, and definitely empty, landscape, such as that exhibited in the western US photographs of Ansel Adams.

Work Cited

Blake, William. "Auguries of Innocence." In *Blake: Complete Writings*, ed. Geoffrey
    Keynes. London: Oxford University Press, 1972.

2

The World Is Your Body
Lionel Rubinoff

Ask of the flowers and they shall teach you the beauty of the earth.
—*St. Francis of Assisi*

The dreadful has already happened.
—*Martin Heidegger*

The End of Nature and the Impoverishment
of the Human Condition

There is a growing consensus among both environmentalists and citizens at large that, as a result of the excesses of consumerism and industrial society, planet earth is facing a serious ecological crisis. Several decades ago, Rachel Carson shocked the general public, as well as many within the scientific community, with her revelations about the effects of industrial pollution and pesticides (especially DDT) on the ecology of the natural environment,[1] while Garrett Hardin sounded the prophetic alarm that we are rapidly approaching a "tragedy of the commons," the condition that occurs when the demands of laissez-faire consumerism and industrial society exceed the carrying capacity of the biosphere.[2] More recently, climatologists have expressed concern over the devastating effects of global warming and global climate change, which is generally thought to be caused by the release of industrially produced greenhouse gases into the atmosphere. The conclusion to which we are forced by these observations is that unless an effort is made to reduce the stress that our contemporary notion of progress is placing upon the natural environment, planet earth will find itself on a collision course with catastrophe. When viewed from the standpoint of political economy, this means replacing our reliance on the human-centred ideology of "the invisible hand" with a more eco-centred conception of "the common good." It means renouncing our Faustian appetite for exponential growth and the uncritical pursuit of the possible—the idea that whatever it is technologically possible to do must be regarded as a moral imperative—in favour of a more Promethean approach that emphasizes the importance of "thoughtfully" measuring progress by the standards of the "common good," which includes the good of nature as well as humanity, rather than by the objectives of the corporate agenda.

Not the least alarming, if not dreadful, consequence of the ecological crisis now facing planet earth is the possibility that we may be on the verge of witnessing both the eclipse or "end" of nature and an impoverishment of the human condition. The possibility of the end of nature is suggested by a variety of recently experienced changes and disruptions in the behaviour and ecology of the natural order, ranging from bizarre weather patterns to unprecedented rates of human-induced species extinction and aberrant reproductive behaviour throughout the animal and plant kingdoms—all of which can be traced to the impact of industrial progress and the encroachment of human settlements upon natural habitats. Increasingly, incidents of such phenomena tend to confirm the extent to which the ecological integrity of the biosphere has been compromised. An equally disturbing source of concern among environmentalists is the fascination we seem to have developed for reinventing nature by means of genetic engineering and other forms of technological manipulation, including the substitution of artificial for natural environments. This results not only in homogenization of landscapes and life forms, but in a reduction of the varieties of physical stimuli upon which , as numerous scholars such as René Dubos, Paul Shepard, and E.O. Wilson have stressed throughout their research and publications, we humans depend for our well-being and for which we appear to have inherited a genetic predisposition.

The hubris with which we engage in the reinvention of physical nature breeds a loss of respect for the sanctity of the pristine nature with which we have co-evolved and within which our very nature qua human has been shaped—with the consequent loss of opportunities for humans to bond with that nature. When respect for pristine nature and the bonding experiences that it makes possible are lost, we are gradually socialized to regard an artificial, man-made nature as an acceptable substitute—as, for exam-

ple, when we regard "plastic trees" as equal, if not superior, to natural trees—
thus breeding the condition described by John Livingston as "the pathology
of urban sensory deprivation" and the perceptual (and thus conceptual)
aberrations that follow from it:

> When perceptual and conceptual aberrations are shared across a soci-
> ety, they may be seen as institutional delusions. There are many of
> these in contemporary society, but none is more important, or more
> ironical, than the belief that high tech urban "progress" (i.e., emanci-
> pation from non-human environmental influences) is a major human
> achievement. R.D. Laing has said, "Human beings seem to have an
> almost unlimited capacity to deceive themselves into taking their own
> lies for truth." It would appear that we have travelled so far in our cul-
> tural self-deceit that we actually believe that we have no need of sen-
> sory stimulation or nutrition beyond that provided by ourselves. No
> need of an influence that is not of human design and fabrication. (Rogue
> Primate 1994, 136)

Deprived of the opportunity to bond with nature, human development is profoundly arrested, with the result, as Paul Shepard warns in Nature and Madness, that the entire culture of humanity is at risk of succumbing to a growing
spread of self-destructiveness.

What makes this concern over the end of nature plausible is the success with which social planners and people in general have been duped into
believing that the idea of nature is nothing more than a social construct.
Thus, for example, in a provocative article entitled "What's Wrong with
Plastic Trees?" Martin Kreiger argues that just as advertising can lead people to value wilderness and nature, so too it can

> create plentiful substitutes.... The demand for rare environments
> is...learned, and conscious public choice can manipulate this learning
> so that the environments which people learn to use and want reflect
> environments that are likely to be available at low cost.... Much more
> can be done with plastic trees and the like to give most people the feel-
> ing that they are experiencing nature. We will have to realize that the
> way in which we experience nature is conditioned by our society—
> which more and more is seen to be receptive to responsible interven-
> tions.[3]

Commenting on these observations, Mark Sagoff points out that, generally speaking, only rich people have the background and leisure to culti-
vate a taste for beautiful environments and only they have the money to

live in and near them. Because rising property values in protected areas drive the poor out, they become increasingly alienated from nature. If, then, the pleasures of the poor were measured equally with those of the rich, as quick as you can say "cost-benefit analysis," there would be parking lots, condominiums, and plastic trees (1974, 210). Tom Regan agrees:

> if a plastic environment can give rise to pleasures equal in value to those arising out of a natural environment, we will have just as much or as little reason to preserve the latter as to manufacture the former. Moreover, if the pleasures flowing from the manufactured environment should happen to outweigh those accompanying the natural environment, we would then have greater reason to enlarge the world of plastic trees and reduce that of living ones. (1982, 195)

Laurence Tribe points out that such a prospect is "the more likely in a society whose social, political, and intellectual tradition regards the satisfaction of individual human wants as the only defensible measure of the good; a tradition that perceives the only legitimate task of reason to be that of consistently identifying and then serving individual appetite, preference, and desire. This tradition is echoed as well in environmental legislation which protects nature not for its own sake but in order to preserve its potential value for man."[4] According to Tribe, the problem is simply that

> By treating individual human need and desire as the ultimate frame of reference, and by assuming that human goals and ends must be taken as externally "given" (whether physiologically, culturally or both) rather than generated by reason, environmental policy makes a value judgment of enormous significance. And once that judgment has been made, any claim for the continued existence of threatened wilderness areas or endangered species must rest on the identification of human wants and needs which would be jeopardized by a disputed development. As our capacity increases to satisfy those needs and wants artificially, the claim becomes tenuous indeed.[5]

The assumption that preferences for artificial environments can easily be cultivated is widespread among economists and developers. Thus, for example, the economist Harry Johnson argues that conservationists and preservationists, obsessed with the impact of development and pollution on the pristine environment, fail to consider the costs and benefits of transforming the environment, and fail to consider as well the possibility of reconstituting the environment (or constructing a new environment catering to

man's environmental desires) from the wealth created by resource exploitation. For Johnson, our ability to transform and reconstruct nature signifies
humanity's superiority over the rest of nature and should be a source of
pride rather than regret—an attitude which is reminiscent of Sophocles's
tribute to humanity's power over nature in his play *Antigone*.

> Many the wonders but nothing walks stranger than man.
> This thing crosses the sea in the winter's storm,
> making his path through the roaring waves.
> And she, the greatest of gods, the Earth—
> deathless she is, and unwearied—he wears her away
> as the ploughs go up and down from year to year
> and his mules turn up the soil.
>
> Gay nations of birds he snares, and leads,
> wild beast tribes and the salty brood of the sea,
> with the twisted mesh of his nets, this clever man.
> He controls with craft the beasts of the open air,
> walkers on hills. The horse with his shaggy mane
> he holds and harnesses, yoked about the neck,
> and the strong bull of the mountain.
>
> Language, and thought like the wind
> and the feelings that make the town,
> he has taught himself, and shelter against the cold,
> refuge from rain. He can help himself.
> He faces no future helpless.[6]

After rejecting as "naive and misleading" the Ricardian assumption that
there is something special about the environment that requires keeping it
intact in its existing form, Johnson, like Sophocles before him, reminds us
that

> Man's whole history has been one of transforming his environment
> rather than accepting its limitations. He has domesticated and raised
> animals for his own use rather than relying on hunting them, and pre-
> viously he invented weapons for hunting them made from pieces of
> the environment rather than relying on his original physical powers.
> He has cleared ground for the planting of crops rather than relying on
> what he could collect from nature's niggardly abundance. And he has
> steadily shifted his economic activities from an overt and direct reliance
> on using products made available by nature to organizing those prod-

ucts, or those sophisticated by human ingenuity, into an industrial productive system which, directly at least, is completely independent of
nature's bounty.[7]

Accordingly, Johnson continues, forests can be replanted, dead lakes can be
revitalized by pumping oxygen into them, or the swimming and fishing
facilities they formerly offered can be replaced by private or public swimming pools and commercial fish farms (1973, 5–6, 8–9). Faced with a choice
between preserving the environment or building a factory, a community
may well decide that, since the factory provides either more employment or
better employment than what is otherwise available, and provides as well
goods that raise people's standards of private living, the benefits from producing and consuming the "goods" outweighs the inconvenience of having
to consume the "bads" as well (1973, 11). Such a choice, Johnson admits, is
more likely to be made in communities suffering from economic hardships
than in affluent communities.

Johnson thus concludes that if a river is being polluted by paper-pulp
production, prohibition of such production or insistence that pulp man-
ufacturers use a non-polluting technology (a form of tax on them) might well
be socially less efficient than a smaller tax on pulp mills, used to provide free
communal parking, swimming pools, and fish ponds, since the former rem-
edy might well benefit the aesthetically rich while depriving the poor of
employment opportunities, while the latter would compensate the poor for
pollution by providing *equivalent* free facilities for recreation (1973, 18).
Notice the emphasis on *equivalent*!

In a similar vein, the atomic physicist Eugene Rabinowitz deplores the
"many rationally unjustifiable things that have been written in recent years—
some by very reputable scientists—about the sacredness of natural ecological systems, their inherent stability and the danger of human interference
with them."[8] Rabinowitz believes that

the only animals whose disappearance may threaten the biological via-
bility of man on earth are the bacteria normally inhabiting our bodies.
For the rest there is no convincing proof that mankind could not survive even as the only animal species on earth. If economical ways could
be developed for synthesizing food from inorganic raw materials—
which is likely to happen sooner or later—man may even be able to
become independent of plants, on which he now depends as sources
for his food. (Schumacher, 1973, 62)

He concludes by pointing out that millions of inhabitants of "city jungles" like New York, Chicago, London, or Tokyo have grown up and spent their whole lives in a practically "azoic" habitat (leaving out rats, mice, cockroaches, and other such obnoxious species) and have survived.

What Kreiger, Johnson, and Rabinowitz are suggesting is that by means of technology it will be possible to substitute a humanly engineered "virtual reality" for the "natural" reality that has evolved through natural selection, without any real sense of loss. For, as William Cronon points out in his introduction to *Uncommon Ground: Toward Reinventing Nature*, the fascinating thing about virtual reality is that, although it initially appears to be the least natural of human creations, the most disembodied and abstracted expression of modernity's alienation from nature, it can in fact serve as a powerful and rather troubling test of whether we really know what we are talking about when we speak of nature. It also, I would add, represents the ultimate surrender to the Faustian appetite for transcendence.

> One would think that the virtual world would stand in pure opposition to the real, but when you put them next to each other this is not nearly so obvious. Yes, a person using computerized sensory apparatus to move through virtual space could hardly be more isolated from the surrounding environment. And yet the better the simulation, the more difficulty we begin to have in distinguishing it from the real. The more engaged we become with experiencing it, the more plausible it begins to be seen as an alternative to the world we know—indeed, an alternative with real advantages. Even more than [a] planned landscape … virtual reality seems to hold out the seductive promise of total control, an environment we can manipulate to our heart's content because it apparently offers no resistance to our fantasies. Some go so far as to imagine that it will ultimately enable us to escape the confines of our own bodies, so that the information in our neurons and synapses can be downloaded in a computer where our mind, our consciousness, our very being can shed its husk of flesh and finally enable us to fulfil the age-old dream of becoming, like the gods, immortal. This is not just science fiction; it is a plausible description of a future in which virtuality will become as real and natural to us as nature is today. (1995, 45)

In such a world there is a very real possibility that the end of nature will have a crippling effect on the quality of human life. For, as I have previously suggested, contrary to what Kreiger, Johnson, and Rabinowitz may believe, there is a growing body of evidence suggesting that were we to engineer such a technological fix, we may end up depriving ourselves of opportunities to experience the "bonding" between humanity and nature, for which humans are phylogenetically disposed and without which humans are not fully human. As Loren Eisley puts it in *The Unexpected Universe*, "for the soul to come to its true self it needs the help and recognition of the dog…. It craves that empathy clinging between man and beast, that nagging shadow of remembrance which, try as we may to deny it, asserts our unity with life and does more. One does not meet oneself until one catches the reflection in *an eye other than human*."[9] The question to be considered, then, is whether the self-deception in which virtual reality has become an acceptable substitute for pristine nature will lead eventually to the eclipse or abolition of a humanity worthy of the human name?

Let us pursue this matter further. If, according to what the Soviet biologist K.M. Khailov has referred to as the "classical evolutionary phylogenetic idea,"[10] the inherent characteristics and needs of all living things are to some extent shaped by their previous evolutionary history, then these inherent characteristics impose limits on adaptability. This idea finds support in the works of René Dubos, John Livingston, Paul Shepard, and, more recently, E.O. Wilson. Each of these writers has seriously explored the proposal that there exists an ingrained need and human affinity for nature. This is the conclusion of what has come to be known as "the biophilia hypothesis" (Kellert and Wilson, 1993).

According to the biophilia hypothesis, what we have traditionally understood as nature, the biologically diverse and independent ecosystem of soils, waters, and organisms with which the human species has co-evolved, is an essential component of the human *Umwelt*—that is to say, the particular niche or world in which it is possible for humans to feel at home. And we may not be capable of adapting successfully to the artificial nature that is gradually taking its place. By impoverishing the source of the stimuli for which we have a primal need, we may at the same time be victimizing ourselves, depriving ourselves of the very thing that makes us human.

Consider! All of the phylogenetic characteristics and processes (metabolic, physiological, and reproductive) of the species have come into existence through actual relationships with other organisms (predators, prey, parasites, disease organisms) as well as with the physical conditions comprising the ecosystem (temperature, radiation, wind, salinity, soil, water). A specimen is, in effect, a summation of its species' historical, adaptive relationship to its environment. In short, a species has the peculiar characteristics it has because those characteristics result from its adaptation to a niche in an ecosystem, which, as Aldo Leopold described it in *A Sand County Almanac*, is a "fountain of energy flowing through a circuit of soils, plants and animals" (1970, 253). This is no less true for humans than for any other species.

The implication of this conception of the economy of nature is that the functioning of all members in their co-evolved ways of life is the source of the integrity of the human niche, or *Umwelt*. The impoverishment of the ecosystem through species extinction will thus impoverish the *umwelt* of humanity, as would the impoverishment of the world of sounds, sights, shapes, and colours lead inevitably to the impoverishment of art and culture.

Central to this holistic conception of nature, as J. Baird Callicott explains in his *In Defense of the Land Ethic,* is a doctrine of internal relations that implies a radically new conception of what it means to be an object, entity, thing, or specimen. From the ecological perspective, relations are not only real but ontologically prior to the relata. At both the organic and microphysical levels of nature, things (organisms and subatomic particles respectively) are what they are because of their relations with other things—that is, with the physical, chemical, and climatic regimes of their niches. Paul Shepard has applied the doctrine of internal relations not only to the human soma but to the human psyche or mind as well. What emerges is a portrait of the mind as an extension of the natural complexity of the ecosystem: the variety of plants and animals and the variety of nerve cells are organic extensions of each other. Nature is a unity, a whole, and contrary to Descartes, the self, the "I," is not only continuous with but constituted by the soma which is Nature. Nature and I are conceptually as well as metaphysically integrated. Or, as Alan Watts has put it, "the world is your body."[11]

Within this holistic conception of the ecosystem it becomes difficult to find support for the dualistic conception of the self and the environment that would justify excluding the non-human from the realm of the morally considerable. In the words of J. Baird Callicott: "In the time-lapse cinematography of imagination one can see oneself arising from the earth, as it were, a pulsating structure in a vast sea of other patterns large and small— some of them mysteriously translating through oneself—finally to be transmuted oneself into the others. The world is, indeed, one's extended body and one's body is the precipitation, the focus of the world in a particular space-time locale" (1983, 113).

Paul Shepard has pointed out, with respect to the cognitive dimension of the human condition, that the most distinctive mark of human consciousness and the *matériel* of human reason are the systems of concepts embodied by human languages. Shepard has suggested that conceptual thought evolved as the taxonomical array of animals and plants was mapped by the emergent consciousness of primate hunter-gatherers. In a very direct way, therefore, human consciousness, including abstract rational thought, is an extension of the environment. From which it would follow, as Arne Naess explains, that the condition of the possibility of achieving maximum human self-realization is the preservation of the maximum level of diversity and symbiosis in nature.

> Self-realization is the realization of the potentialities of life. Organ-
> isms that differ from each other in three ways give us less diversity
> than organisms that differ from each other in one hundred ways. There-
> fore, the self-realization we experience when we identify with the uni-
> verse is heightened by an increase in the number of ways in which
> individuals, societies, and even species and life forms realize them-
> selves. The greater the diversity, the greater the Self-realization. (1993,
> 185)

For Shepard, these observations are sufficient to secure an argument for species conservation: if we simplify and impoverish the earth's ecosystems, we risk rendering future generations of human beings mentally degenerate. Lacking a rich and complex natural environment to support a rich and complex intelligence—as correspondent, analogue, and stimulus—human intelligence may simply atrophy.[12] As Shepard writes,

> the substitution of a limited number of genetically deformed and phe-
> notypically confusing species for the wild fauna may, through impaired
> perception, degrade the human capacity for self-knowledge. The loss
> of metaphorical distance between ourselves and wild animals and the
> incorporation of domestic animals as slaves in human society alter
> ourselves and our cosmos. Without distance and difference, the others
> remain monsters of a terrifying jungle or, dissolved in our own uncon-
> scious minds, monsters of a chaotic and undifferentiated self.[13]

The fact of our having evolved in natural communities, explains Shepard, constitutes a kind of phylogenetic felicity in which we acknowledge that the fish, amphibian, mammal, and primate are still alive within us and therefore have a double existence. They are present as bits of DNA, affirming kinship, and also in the world around us as independent others. Or, as Lewis Thomas explains as he reflects on the host of small micro-organisms that inhabit the cells of his own body:

There they are moving about in my cytoplasm.... They are much less closely related to me than they are to each other and to the free living bacteria out under the hill. They feel like strangers, but the thought comes that the same creatures, precisely the same, are out there in the cells of sea-gulls, and whales, and dune grass, and seaweed, and hermit crabs, and further inland in the leaves of the beech in my backyard, and in the family of skunks beneath the back fence, and even in that fly on the window. Through them, I am connected: I have close relatives, once removed, all over the place. (1990, 57)

According to Shepard, it is on the basis of such considerations that we can begin to liberate ourselves from captivity to the Cartesian dualism which has alienated us from both nature and ourselves. Or, in the words of J. Baird Callicott:

If the world is one's body, and not only does one's consciousness image in its specific content the world around, but the very structure of one's psyche and rational faculties are formed through adaptive interaction with the ecological organization of nature, then one's self, both physically and psychologically, merges in a gradient from its central core outwardly into the environment. (1983, 114)

Elizabeth Atwood Lawrence agrees, when she speculates that since language continually adapts to changing conditions in an evolutionary process that has been compared to biological evolution,

It is difficult to predict the ways in which our diminishing interactions with the natural world and different perceptions of animals will affect future expressions of cognitive biophilia.... If we continue our current policy of destructiveness toward nature, does this mean that language will contain fewer and fewer symbolic references to animals—with consequent impoverishment of thought and expression? (1993, 336–37)

It can be further argued that what is at stake is not only the integrity of our cognitive faculties, but our mental health and the very possibility of experiencing a meaningful and more personally rewarding human existence. In the words of René Dubos, an early proponent of the biophilia hypothesis:

Conservation is based on human value systems; its deepest significance is the human situation and the human heart.... The cult of wilderness is not a luxury; it is a necessity for the preservation of mental health.... Above and beyond the economic ... reasons for conservation, there are aesthetic and moral ones which are even more compelling.... We are shaped by the earth. The characteristics of the environment in which we develop condition our biological and mental being and the quality of our life. Were it only for selfish reasons, therefore, we must maintain variety and harmony in nature. (*Ecology and Religion in History*, 1969, 129)

Indeed, as Hugh Iltis has suggested, concern over our mental, psychic, and physical well-being may represent a far more compelling basis for nature conservation than the mere rationalization of enhanced material benefit.

Here, finally, is an argument for nature preservation free of purely [material] considerations; not just clean air because polluted air gives cancer; not just pure water because polluted water kills the fish we might like to catch; ... but preservation of the natural ecosystem to give body and soul a chance to function in the way they were selected to function in their original phylogenetic home.... Could it be that the stimuli of non-human living diversity make the difference between sanity and madness? We may expect that science will [someday] furnish the objective proofs of suppositions about man's needs for a living environment which we, at present, can only guess at through timid intuition; that one of these days we shall find the intricate neurological bases of why a leaf or a lovely flower affects us so very differently than a broken beer bottle. (1973, 19)

When viewed from the perspective of the biophilia hypothesis, an injury to nature may thus be regarded as an injury to oneself. Or, as Leopold puts it, "one of the penalties of an ecological education is that one lives in a world of wounds" (1970, 197). A report in *Time* in 2000 concludes with the question, "How long will earth be a hospitable place for humanity when it is no longer a fit home for our next-of-kin?"[14]

Thus do ecology and an informed ecological consciousness give new meaning and new substance to "enlightened self-interest," and thereby facilitate the transformation of egocentrism into eco-centric environmentalism. Through the pursuit of enlightened, eco-centred self-interest, inspired by the liberation of biophilia, the discourse and politics of a techno-culture in the grip of an ethic of domination will give way to the language, poetry, and politics of an eco-culture devoted to the celebration rather than domination of nature. The preservation of biodiversity, and the human experience of it, are the *sine qua non* not simply of a continuing human presence on the planet earth but of a continuing presence worthy of the human name, and thus worthy of the celebration of poets and artists for whom to be human is to be committed to the guardianship of the earth as a condition of human self-making.

Self-Realization and Biophilia

Precisely this conception of enlightened self-interest finds expression in the Greek legend in which the giant Antaeus retained his strength only while in direct contact with the earth. For this reason he was readily overpowered by Hercules when his two feet were off the ground. Commenting on this legend, René Dubos writes, "because man is still of the earth, he too loses attributes essential to his survival when he allows the technological way of life to dissociate him completely from the natural environment."

> If men were to colonize the moon or Mars—even with abundant supplies of oxygen, water and food, as well as adequate protection against heat, cold and radiation—they would not long retain their humanness, because they would be deprived of those stimuli which only the earth can provide. Similarly, we shall progressively lose our humanness on earth, if we continue to pour filth into the atmosphere; to befoul soil, lakes, and rivers; to disfigure landscapes with junk piles; to destroy the wild plants and animals that do not contribute to monetary values; and thus to transform the globe into an environment alien to our evolutionary past. The quality of human life is inextricably woven with the kinds and variety of stimuli man receives from the earth and the life it harbours, because human nature is shaped biologically and mentally by external nature. (*A God Within*, 1972, 38)

John Livingston observes, with respect to what he calls "the sensory deprivation in civilized society" and the extraordinary boom in the houseplant business that for him symbolizes the extent of the urban problem:

> To be alive means to be sensate means to be *in touch*. We have to maintain contact with something—anything—that is *alive*. It's the most fundamental part of being. The geranium on the tenement window is both an offering to the mysterious tidal pull of some distant biological memory, and a heartbreaking cry for help. (*The Fallacy of Wildlife Conservation*, 1981, 94)

In short, the end of nature and the end of humanity go hand in hand; not in the sense that there will no longer be biologically functioning human animals procreating and inhabiting a world of natural processes in the future; it is rather, as I have stressed throughout this essay, that we risk the possibility of a world in which there will no longer be a human presence worthy of the human name.[15] And what is even more repugnant is the possibility of the eclipse of even the memory of such a human presence, including the memory of what it was like to live within a nature whose integrity was still intact.

What we will have lost in the desacralized, post-natural world into which we seem to be heading is that mysterious, subtle, and inherently incomprehensible dimension of a nature that exists beyond the domination of human interference and reason, beyond the domination that takes the form of even understanding, let alone controlling, exploitation and so-called wise management. As the Nobel Prize laureate Barbara McClintock often emphasized, nature is characterized by a complexity that vastly exceeds the capacities of the human imagination. Organisms have a life and order of their own that even scientists can only begin to fathom. "They do everything we [can think of]," she writes, "they do it better, more efficiently, more marvellously."[16] Speaking as a scientist, McClintock has come to realize that there is a creative force that is both immanent in the process of evolution and yet transcendent to our understanding. Or, as Steven Hawking put it, in response to Einstein's stubborn insistence that "God does not play dice with the universe," not only does God play dice, he "sometimes throws them where they can't be seen" (1994, 113, 70).

For Einstein, the fact that the universe was rigidly determined was a source of security and comfort; it was also an indispensable condition of sustaining the mythic belief that it could be brought entirely under human control. For McClintock and Hawking, the discovery that creation is full of surprises is a source of humility and an occasion for celebrating the existence of that mysterious dimension that lies beyond our control and yet is the source of the gift of life itself. Accordingly, the experience of wild nature is both mysterious and ennobling. What gives this experience, or adventure of humanity, its true depth of meaning is the experiencing of a nature that is not just for the taking and benefit of humanity, but exists somewhere beyond our reach. Once again we are made to understand that, fugitive though the instant may be in which this encounter with mystery occurs, the spirit of humanity is, during it, ennobled by a genuine moment of emotional dignity.

It was no doubt such experiences that led Aldo Leopold to the question: "Was the earth made for man's use or has man merely the privilege of temporarily possessing an earth made for other and inscrutable purposes?"[17] The question of what he can properly do with it must, according to Leopold, necessarily be affected by this question. Regrettably, in the artificial and mechanically determined nature that we have created, we are distracted from even noticing the absence of that mysterious and inherently incomprehensible dimension. We are distracted by the fascination and intoxication that we have acquired for the major scientific and industrial achievements of modern society. We are intoxicated by these achievements and the optimism to which they have given rise because they have increased our power over nature and even life itself, and have thus increased our ability to control the future. As one aspiring techno-manager puts it, it is time for us "as incipient planet managers, to use this power, and use it well.... The ancient Greeks, the Renaissance communities, the founders of America, the Victorians, enjoyed no such challenge as this. What a time to be alive."[18]

The author of this statement is the well-known and highly regarded naturalist, Norman Myers. He greets the potential inherent in the technology of both genetic and planetary engineering with great optimism, because he believes that by means of these technologies we can protect and improve upon nature's bounty—as if it should be left to human technology to complete and fulfil the goals of natural selection.

As Elizabeth Dodson Gray points out, this patriarchal conception of stewardship—the subject of previously considered objections—is inherent in the Western tradition and can be traced back to the Old Testament.[19] Sadly, in a techno-culture such as ours, the technology by means of which stewardship is undertaken is not likely to facilitate the opportunity for nature to enjoy a flourishing existence. It is more likely to enslave and degrade nature. In short, as Dodson Gray and Livingston rightly complain, in the techno-culture, stewardship turns out to be just another version of the ethic and discourse of domination. For again, even though we are in divine service on earth, we are, by virtue of our captivity to the Faustian ideology of the technological a priori, unquestionably in charge. In the techno-culture the assumption remains, as Livingston puts it, "that all of wild nature is a herd, a flock, a crop, to be manipulated and controlled in the public, national and human interest."

> Man is total proprietor, manager, and decision-maker with respect to wildlife. This is the clear-cut and unambiguous message of "good hus-

bandry" conservation. Wildlife is yours; yours to manipulate in your own best interest. If you treat it badly or stupidly, only you (not wildlife) will be the loser; if you treat it well, it is yours from which to profit in perpetuity. (*The Fallacy of Wildlife Conservation*, 1981, 26)

This is referred to by Dodson Gray as "Adam's" point of view, which is not only patriarchal but inherently Faustian. The citizens of Adam's world tend to greet the technologies of planetary control with great optimism, because they offer us the most hope of continuing our present way of life, our economic growth, and our habits of consumption without our having seriously to question the foundations and values upon which this lifestyle has been built. Technology promises us a way to survive in almost any environment we may create. But while its promise is indeed a promise of progress and utopia, it is also, I fear, a promise spoken *in nomine diaboli*.

Conclusion: Quo Vadis?

The outstanding scientific discovery of the twentieth century
is not television, or radio, but rather the complexity
of the land organism.
—*Aldo Leopold*

To lament the end of nature, in the spirit of Paul Shepard, Bill McKibben, and the many others who have argued the case for wilderness preservation, does not imply acceptance of what William Cronon has aptly described as the *reductio ad absurdum* of deep ecology: the view that "if wild nature is the only thing worth saving, and if our mere presence destroys it, then the sole solution to our own unnaturalness, the only way to protect sacred wilderness from profane humanity, would be to commit suicide" (1995, 83). Notwithstanding the importance for the human imagination of the idea of nature as a pristine wilderness free of human interference, and granted the continuing human need for exposure to stimuli that only pristine nature can provide, it is equally important to recognize, as Cronon and his colleagues point out in *Uncommon Ground* (1995, 34), that the idea of nature—including the idea of pristine nature—is, to some extent, a human and social construction, reflecting historically conditioned values and modes of human self-understanding. To acknowledge this does not mean that the idea of nature is nothing more than a purely human artifact constructed in accordance with the subjectivist principle that *esse est percipi*. Cronon's appeal to the sociology of knowledge is prompted by a concern with those who insist on holding on to an overly romanticized and outdated image of nature as a wilderness devoid of a human presence, or at least devoid of a presence actively engaged in the cultivation and use of nature. For those like Cronon who believe that it is possible for pristine nature to both accommodate an active human presence and indeed flourish because of it, it does not follow that nature must lose that mysterious dimension that is the source of its majesty and independence. Cronon, and indeed most environmentalists who subscribe to the main tenets of Aldo Leopold's land ethic, would thus agree with Michael Pollan when he argues that, whereas it might have made sense for Thoreau to propose that "in wildness is the preservation of the world," given the present state of the natural environment, we might be forced to the conclusion that, as Wendell Berry suggests, "in human culture is the preservation of wildness."[20] In the world in which we currently live the idea of pristine nature not only does not exclude a human presence, it may actually require an active presence of precisely the sort envisaged by Leopold in his vision of the land ethic.

In short, it is too late now to do nothing and simply withdraw from actively engaging with wild nature. If wild nature is to be rescued from the unfortunate impact that unconstrained technological and industrial progress has had upon it, it will require the intervention of what Michael Pollan refers to as a "green thumb." The green thumb is "the gardener who can nimbly walk in line between the dangers of over and under-cultivation, between pushing nature too far, and giving her too much ground. His garden is a place where her ways and his designs are brought gracefully into alignment."[21] For Pollan, the green thumb is the metaphor that marries the natural and the human power.

Given the urgency of the need for a green thumb, it is unlikely that defenders of the wild can meaningfully exclude humanity from playing a role in the restoration of ecological integrity. Moreover, as Murray Bookchin, Michael Pollan, and even René Dubos have been at pains to explain, both the human appreciation of nature and human manipulation of nature are themselves "natural" phenomena—as natural as the conduct displayed by the rest of the living creatures who co-inhabit the natural environment.[22] Even such an eloquent and forceful voice in defence of the wild as Holmes Rolston III insists that proponents of wilderness preservation do not mean to deep-freeze the present ecosystem. Despite their preservationist vocabulary, their care for the bio-systemic welfare allows for alternative management and use. We are not, according to Holmes Rolston, "committed to what nature has made of itself on its own resources as the best of all possible ecosystems; it may well be that the role of man—at once 'citizen' and 'king'—is to govern what has hitherto been the partial success of the evolutionary process."[23] In short, though we revere the earth, we may yet "humanize it."

At the same time, as René Dubos argues, given the conditions under which we currently inhabit the biosphere, we must realize that, in the long run, the world's good coincides with humanity's own most meaningful good, and that "man can manipulate nature to his best interest only if he first loves her for her own sake" (1972, 45). In human-nature, and human-human relationships, each partner may be understood to facilitate or midwife the potential of the other. With respect to the human-nature relationships, the human agent is like an artist who recognizes the forms inherent in nature and helps to realize their expression in works of art, so that, in a very meaningful sense, without the artist, what nature is in its essence remains unfulfilled. Herein, as John Passmore explains, lies the wisdom of the *Hermetica Asclepius*, written in the second century: "God willed that the universe should not be complete until man had done his part. Man does not complete the universe simply by being in it. He helps to create it."[24] In this process, not to be confused with patriarchal domination from "Adam's point of view," there is unquestionably a role to be played by what E.F. Schumacher has aptly described as "appropriate technology" or "technology with a human face" (1973, Part III, chap. 5).

Yet, as Schumacher, Aldo Leopold, René Dubos, Garrett Hardin, and Murray Bookchin, to name only a few, have stressed throughout their writings, there are limits to how far the biosphere can tolerate the manipulation of nature in the service of human interests. As in human-human relationships, in human-nature relationships there is a point at which the dominant partner ceases to be a partner in the act of creation and becomes instead an agent of domination. This can happen when the human agent becomes possessed with a Faustian and demonic appetite to imprison the weaker partner into a master-servant relationship—often disguised as an expression of the "wise-use" of nature in the service of such noble ends as progress and the improvement of mankind; precisely the ideology of resource exploitation, or "resourcism," as espoused by the likes of Clifford Pinchot, Harry Johnson, Leonard Kreiger, and Julian Simon.[25]

It is at this point that the intoxicating spell and rhetoric of the technological a priori is spoken *in nomine diaboli*. The burden of our lament and *crie de coeur* over the end of nature, and E.O. Wilson's appeal to the biophilia hypothesis in the name of species preservation and diversification, is to force us to rethink the question of limits with respect to both the extent of our encroachment upon wilderness and the nature of what might be regarded as an appropriate form of technological manipulation of nature. Through such reflections we may hopefully purge ourselves of our Faustian appetites and resume our more "natural" roles as citizen-gardeners, rather than as conquerors, in keeping with the true nature of our evolutionary history. In the words of Michael Pollan, "the habit of bluntly opposing nature and culture has only gotten us into trouble, and we won't work ourselves free of this trouble until we have developed a more complicated and supple sense of how we fit into nature" (1991, 97). Gardening, explains Pollen, tutors us in nature's ways, fostering an ethic of reciprocity, of give-and-take with respect to the land. Gardens teach the necessary lesson that "there might be some middle ground between human culture and the forest—between those who would complete the conquest of the planet in the name of progress, and those who believe it's time we abdicated our rule and left the world in the care of its more innocent species. The garden suggests there might be a place where we can meet nature half way" (1991, 64).

Notes

1 Rachel Carson, *Silent Spring* (Boston: Houghton Mifflin, 1962). For more recent exposures of the effects of industrial pollutants on the fertility, intelligence, and survival of the human and other species of living organisms, see Theo Colborn, Dianne Dumanoski, and John Peterson Myers, *Our Stolen Future* (New York: Dutton, 1996), and Deborah Cadbury, *The Feminization of Nature* (London: Hamish Hamilton, 1996).

2 Garrett Hardin, "The Tragedy of the Commons," *Science* 162 (13 December 1968): 1243–48.

3 Martin Kreiger, *Science* 179 (1973): 446–55.

4 Laurence Tribe, "Ways Not to Think about Plastic Trees," *Yale Law Journal* 83, 7 (June 1974). Reprinted in Donald Van DeVeer and Christine Pierce, eds., *People, Penguins and Plastic* (Belmont, CA: Wadsworth, 1986), 255.

5 Ibid. Tribe cites the following advertisement by Monsanto as a case in point: "At last, the work-free poolside! Simply install Round-the-Home Astro Turf ... it gives your poolside the look of lush grass, right up to the water's edge. Besides being bright, beautiful, durable and fade resistant, Round-the-Home Astro Turf is also easy to maintain—simply wash it with a hose" (260n11).

6 Sophocles, *Antigone*, trans. Elizabeth Wycoff, in David Greene and Richard Lattimore, eds., *The Complete Greek Tragedies*, vol. 2 (Chicago: University of Chicago Press, 1959), ll. 335–59.

7 Harry Johnson, *Man and His Environment* (London: British North American Committee, 1973), 5. Johnson's approach to development is in essence the same as that taken by Clifford Pinchot for whom development is both an obligation as well as a patriotic duty. "The first principle of conservation," writes Pinchot, "is

development, the use of the natural resources now existing on this continent for the benefit of the people who live here now. There may be as much waste in neglecting the development and use of certain natural resources as there is in their destruction…. The development of our natural resources and the fullest use of them for the present generation is the first duty of this generation…. The first duty of the human race is to control the earth it lives upon." (*The Fight for Conservation*, 1910; cited in Walter Levey and Christopher Hallowell, eds., *Green Perspectives*. New York: Harper Collins, 1994, 81–86). A similar attitude toward nature and humanity's relationship to it finds expression in the thought of the economist Rexford G. Tugwell, an influential advisor to American president Franklin Delano Roosevelt. "A part of the conspicuous victory over nature on this continent," writes Tugwell, "has been the power which has been exhibited in subduing natural materials and forces to a will for well-being. Nature has been reduced to order, to regimentation. This is a process which should have freed men as it enslaved nature" (*The Battle for Democracy*, New York: Columbia University Press, 1935, 195). More recently, Charles Krauthammer makes precisely the same point when he declares that a "sane environmentalism … begins by unashamedly declaring that nature is here to serve man…. Nature is not our ward. It is not our master. It is to be respected and even cultivated. But it is man's world. And when man has to choose between his well-being and that of nature, nature will have to accommodate" (*Time*, June 17, 1994, 64). Such attitudes reflect the continuing influence of the Lockean and Baconian philosophies of nature. Locke argued that since "God gave the world to Men … for their benefit and the greatest conveniences of life they were capable to draw from it … it cannot be supposed he meant it should always remain … uncultivated. He gave it to the use of the industrious and rational." (*Second Treatise of Government*, Book II, chap. 5, Sect. 34). For Bacon, nature had to be "hounded in her wanderings," "bound into service," and made a "slave." She was to be "put in constraint" and the aim of the scientist was to "torture nature's secrets from her." For more detailed discussions of how Locke's views and Bacon's metaphors may be interpreted, see L. Rubinoff, "Beyond the Domination of Nature," *Alternatives* 12, 2 (Winter 1985); Carolyn Merchant, *The Death of Nature* (New York: Harper & Row, 1980); and William Leiss, *The Domination of Nature* (New York: George Braziller, 1972), chap. 3.

8 Eugene Rabinowitz, the *Times* (London), April 29, 1972. Cited by E.F. Schumacher, *Small Is Beautiful* (New York: Harper & Row, 1973, 1989), 110.

9 Loren Eisley, *The Unexpected Universe* (New York: Harcourt, Brace & World, 1969), 24. Alienation from nature, and the subsequent loss of the opportunity to bond with it, is one of the major consequences of humanity's attempt to conquer nature. Of equal concern is the problem raised by C.S. Lewis, who points out that "what we call Man's power over Nature turns out to be a power exercised by some men over other men with Nature as its instrument … Man's conquest of Nature, if the dreams of some scientific planners are realized, means the rule of a few hundreds of men over billions upon millions of men…. The final stage is come when Man by eugenics, by prenatal conditioning, and by an education and prop-

aganda based on a perfect applied psychology, has obtained full control over himself. *Human* nature will be the last part of nature to surrender to Man.... For the power of Man to make himself what he pleases ... means the power of some men to make other men what *they* please," with the result, according to Lewis, that they are no longer human; they are artifacts. Man's final conquest, according to Lewis, will thus prove to be "the abolition of man." Furthermore, Lewis continues to argue, the conditioners themselves, no longer controlled by wisdom and moral values, will become slaves to their own pleasures and impulses, dictated not by reason but by chance, that is to say, by irrational Nature. "At the moment, then, of man's victory over Nature, we find the whole human race subjected to some individual men, and those individuals subjected to that in themselves which is purely 'natural'—to their irrational impulses. Nature, untrammeled by values, rules the Conditioners and, through them, all humanity. Man's conquest of Nature turns out in the moment of its consummation, to be Nature's conquest of Man." "The Abolition of Man," in Herman Daly, ed., *Economics, Ecology, Ethics* (San Francisco: W.H. Freeman, 1980), 177–87.

10 K.M. Khailov, "The Problem of Systematic Organization in Theoretical Biology," in Walter Buckley, ed., *Modern Systems Research for the Behavioural Scientist* (Chicago: Aldine, 1968), 47, 48. See also, Gerald Royce, "Beyond Economics," *Canadian Forum* (February 1973).

11 Alan Watts, *The Book on the Taboo against Knowing Who You Are* (New York: Pantheon, 1966). See also, Paul Shepard, "Ecology and Man: A Viewpoint," in P. Shepard and Daniel McKinley, eds., *The Subversive Science* (Boston: Houghton Mifflin, 1969). For J. Baird Callicott's discussion of the doctrine of internal relations, see his *In Defense of the Land Ethic* (Albany: State University of New York Press, 1993), chap. 6.

12 Paul Shepard, "Ecology and Man: A Viewpoint," in P. Shepard and Daniel McKinley, eds., *The Subversive Science* (Boston: Houghton Mifflin, 1969). See also Callicott, 113.

13 Paul Shepard, "On Animal Friends," in S.R. Kellert and E.O. Wilson, eds., *The Biophilia Hypothesis* (Washington, DC: Island Press), 298.

14 *Time*, January 17, 2000, 36.

15 See Hans Jonas, "Technology and Responsibility: Reflections on the New Task of Ethics," in H. Jonas, *Philosophical Essays* (Englewood Cliffs, NJ: Prentice-Hall, 1974), and H. Jonas, *The Imperative of Responsibility* (Chicago: University of Chicago Press, 1984).

16 Barbara McClintock, cited by Evelyn Fox Keller, "Women and Basic Research: Respecting the Unexpected," *Technology Review* (November/December, 1984): 46.

17 Aldo Leopold, "Conservation as a Moral Issue," in Donald Scherer and Thomas Attig, eds., *Ethics and the Environment* (Englewood Cliffs, NJ: Prentice-Hall, 1983), 11.

18 Norman Myers, cited by Bill McKibben in "The End of Nature," in *The New Yorker* (September 1979), reprinted in *Earth News* (Spring 1990), 3. A book-length version of this essay was published in 1989 by Random House under the same title.

19 Elizabeth Dodson Gray, *Green Paradise Lost* (Wellesley, MA: Roundtable Press, 1981).

20 Wendell Berry, cited by Michael Pollan in *Second Nature* (New York: Atlantic Monthly Press, 1991), 135. By culture, Berry means one inspired by what he refers to as an "agrarian vision," which derives from a proper understanding of the relationship between our bodies and the earth, the importance of this relationship to the health of our souls, and a healthy respect for the rituals of an organically based and ecologically informed practice of agriculture or farming which takes the form of a dialogue with the earth and by means of which we might hope to facilitate a recovery of the earth from the assault of modern industry and agribusiness. For a more detailed exposition of Berry's agrarian vision see *The Art of the Commonplace: The Agrarian Essays of Wendell Berry*, Norman Wirzba, ed. (Washington, DC: Shoemaker & Hoard, 2002). The quotation from Thoreau comes from an essay entitled "Walking," which may be found in Carl Bode, ed., *The Portable Thoreau*, rev. ed. (New York: Penguin, 1980), 609.

21 Pollan, *Second Nature*, 124. See also, 147-48. For other uses of the metaphor of the garden in developing an environmental ethic, see J. Baird Callicott, op. cit., 136-39, and René Dubos, "A Theology of the Earth," in Ian G. Barbour, ed., *Western Man and Environmental Ethics* (Reading, MA: Addison-Wesley, 1973).

22 This point is well developed by Murray Bookchin in his "What Is Social Ecology" in M. Zimmerman et al., eds. (Englewood Cliffs, NJ: Prentice Hall, 1993), 354-73.

23 Holmes Rolston III, "Is There an Ecological Ethic?" in Donald Scherer and Thomas Attig, eds., op. cit., 53. Rolston's approach in this essay incorporates much of the approach taken by Aldo Leopold in his landmark publication, *A Sand County Almanac*, originally published by Oxford University Press in 1949 and reissued by Oxford in 1968 and by Ballantine Books in 1970.

24 Cited by John Passmore in *Man's Responsibility for Nature* (New York: Charles Scribner's Sons, 1974), 33.

25 In addition to the references to Pinchot, Kreiger, Tugwell, and Johnson elsewhere in this essay (esp. note 7, above), see Julian Simon, *Population Matters* (New Brunswick, NJ: Transaction, 1990), and Julian Simon, *The Ultimate Resource*, (Princeton, NJ: Princeton University Press, 1981). Simon's publications arguably comprise the most influential of all recent attempts to defend the ideology of resourcism.

Works Cited

Callicott, J. Baird. *In Defense of the Land Ethic*. Albany: State University of New York Press, 1983.

Cronon, William. *Uncommon Ground: Toward Reinventing Nature*. New York: W.W. Norton, 1995.

Dodson Gray, Elizabeth. *Green Paradise Lost*. Wellesley, MA: Roundtable, 1981.

Dubos, René. *Ecology and Religion in History*. New York: Oxford University Press, 1969.

————. *A God Within*. New York: Scribner's, 1972.

Hawking, Stephen. *Black Holes, Baby Universes*. New York: Bantam, 1994.

Iltis, Hugh. "Can One Love a Plastic Tree?" *Bulletin of the Ecological Society of America* 54(1973): 5–7.

Johnson, Harry. *Man and His Environment*. London: British North American Committee, 1973.

Kellert, S.R., and E.O. Wilson, eds. *The Biophilia Hypothesis*. Washington, DC: Island Press, 1993.

Lawrence, Elizabeth Atwood. "The Sacred Bee, the Filthy Pig, and the Bat Out of Hell: Animal Symbolism as Cognitive Biophilia." In *The Biophilia Hypothesis*, ed. Kellert and Wilson.

Leopold, Aldo. *A Sand County Almanac with Essays on Conservation from Round River*. New York: Ballantine, 1970.

Livingston, John. *Rogue Primate*. Toronto: Key Porter, 1994.

————. *The Fallacy of Wildlife Conservation*. Toronto: McClelland & Stewart, 1981.

Naess, Arne. "Simple in Means, Rich in Ends." In *Environmental Philosophy: From Animal Rights to Radical Ecology*, ed. M. Zimmerman et al. Englewood Cliffs, NJ: Prentice Hall, 1993.

Pollan, Michael. *Second Nature*. New York: Atlantic Monthly Press, 1991.

Regan, Tom. "The Nature and Possibility of an Environmental Ethic." *In All That Dwell Therein*. Berkeley, CA: University of California Press, 1982.

Sagoff, Mark. "On Preserving the Natural Environment." *Yale Law Journal* 84, 2 (1974).

Schumacher, E.F. *Small Is Beautiful*. New York: Harper & Row, 1973, 1989.

Shepard, Paul. *Nature and Madness*. San Francisco: Sierra Club, 1982.

Thomas, Lewis. *A Long Line of Cells*. New York: Book of the Month Club, 1990.

3

Growing Roots in Nature

Karen Krug

For the first seventeen years of my life, I lived on a farm in Saskatchewan. Although I have since spent more than this length of time in urban centres of Canada, growing up on a prairie farm has indelibly shaped my life and my attitude toward the environment. I developed an appreciation for the natural world, and a deeply rooted love for the prairie. Now working in urbanized southern Ontario, I continue to long for my childhood experience of living in daily communion with the land and the sky. In coming to terms with my rural experience, however, I have gone through various stages of awareness. Tracing the major developments in my evolution of understanding about agrarian life and the formation of environmental consciousness has led me to some ideas about how to recover the positive connection between agrarian lifestyles and environmental consciousness.

Idealism

My first impression of the impact agrarian life has on environmental consciousness is best described as idealistic. However, as the examples below will make clear, this idealistic viewpoint emerges from an agrarian lifestyle that may no longer be widely accessible. For instance, when I was young, my father farmed using a small tractor without a cab. So close to nature was he from this vantage point that one day he reached up as a sandpiper flew by and caught it in his hand. On occasion he would spot a nest of eggs, abandoned ducklings, or young rabbits, and all of us kids would head out to see such treasures. Many weekend or summer days, we would pack lunches and travel to whatever field Dad was working (seeding, summer-fallowing, or harvesting), then explore the local bluff for the day, playing hide-and-seek in the sweeping fields of grain or the overgrown grass of the abandoned farmyards. Until I left the farm to attend university, I wasn't conscious of the strong sense of place that developed in me as I spent hot, dry summers roaming the fields and exploring bluffs, and cold but sunny winters building fortresses against blizzards or cross-country skiing over frozen expanses of prairie. Only upon returning from away did I begin to comprehend the privilege of falling asleep in a silence broken solely by the sounds of night creatures and the elements; of looking up to a sky punctu-ated by a million tiny pinpricks of stars or dominated by a harvest moon; of being able to see the sun rise or set across a heavenly palette every sin-gle day. On my trips home during my university years, I would reconnect with the prairie as I roamed the fields, calling into the wind and releasing fierce tears of longing. Emblazoned in my memory is an image from a time when I took to the fields following a string of minus-forty-degree days and came upon a rabbit emerging from hiding to sun himself and do calisthenics in the glistening snow. Now, when I return "home" with my three-year-old daughter, we share with grandparents the thrill of watching beavers, geese, and goslings, deer, rabbits, and other creatures who frequent this landscape.

For me, the farm is still home, despite the fact that I have not lived there during my adult life. Ownership has bought the privilege of inhabit-ing this place free of intrusion by others. Although I recognize how pre-sumptuous it is to buy and sell nature's spaces as our own, my experience confirms that long-term tenure provides the opportunity for development of a deeply rooted sense of place. I wholeheartedly agree with Edmund O'Sullivan, who maintains that, "In a time when the global economy can no longer be relied upon to provide the basic necessities of life, the cultivation of a sense of place has built within it a corrective to the vagaries of global-ization" (1999, 246). Sharon Butala, writing about her experience moving to a ranch in southern Saskatchewan, recognizes how the place itself changed her consciousness: "Slowly, through my joy in the beauty of this new land-scape, I began to learn new things, to see my life differently. I began to real-ize how life for all of us in the West is informed and shaped by Nature in ways that we don't even realize, much less notice consciously" (1994, xv).

Factors such as the relative isolation, the lack of dependency upon exter-nal material goods, the permanent connection to land and sky throughout the seasons, and the inevitable interactions with and against nature led me to understand how I am both a part of and apart from nature. While my peers in urban centres or towns may have had access to diverse intellectual, athletic, musical, and recreational activities to which I did not, what I lacked in such opportunities was more than compensated for by a richness of awareness—specifically the ability to see diversity where others saw emptiness or monotony. This ability to see richness and complexity in a land where many see relatively little is poignantly described in a poem by Margaret Laurence. Crossing Canada by train, the speaker in the poem meets a passenger bound for Vancouver. In response to this traveller's request to tell her when they reach more interesting scenery, the speaker remarks that she is from the prairies and for her this *is* the more interesting countryside.

The humbleness that comes with daily reminders of one's dependence upon the natural world, combined with the ability to delight at the unexpected beauty or pleasures of nature, seems missing from the lives of those who have grown up less directly connected to nature and with ready access to human-constructed goods. To see diversity even in apparent monotony, to live simply and humbly while appreciating nature are essential characteristics required for conservation—all of which seem to be supported by an agrarian lifestyle. However, this idealistic portrayal of agrarian life does not represent the full picture.

Pragmatism

There is not consensus about whether agriculture plays a positive role in shaping relations to the natural world. Butala contrasts urban and country[1] sensibilities concerning Nature, reinforcing the more positive view. As part of the country experience, she recollects "a combination of smells, the feel of the air, a sense of the presence of Nature as a living entity around me" (1994, 9). By contrast, in her city-dwelling years, she remembers acquiring a different understanding, typical of that held by urban people, of nature as "a place to holiday—the mountains, the seaside, a quiet lake somewhere in the country—as a place to acquire a suntan, have a summer romance, paint a picture of, enjoy a change of atmosphere" (1994, 9). Butala's experience leads her to believe that being raised in nature, or living with very little separation between oneself and nature, leaves one with a different understanding of what nature is. These contrasting perceptions of nature are also identified by Stan Rowe in a book of his essays reflecting on agriculture and ecology. Although Rowe's distinction concerning the two ways of perceiving nature is very similar to Butala's, for him the delineating factors are not urban versus country, but rather stem from people's intent and attitude: "Sometime soon we will recognize the difference between going to a native grassland to sit and listen and learn from a microcosm of the World, to open ourselves to it for inspiration as to how best to live with it and minister to it, and going there with the intention of turning it into a show place for wild animals, into a landscape painting, into a pasture for cattle or—most terrible thought—into just another wheat field" (1990, 14).

In Rowe's ethic, utilitarian uses—including both farming and ranching—interfere with the development of appropriate relations with nature. In stark contrast, a farmer interviewed by Diane Baltaz in a study on the spirituality of farming implies that it is precisely the utilitarian relationship that leads to closeness with nature: "This closeness to nature is spiritual, and I can't just get it by walking through the bush, but [rather] by working with nature. In farming, the touch and smell of the earth gives me this awareness" (1991, 61–62). For this farmer (incidentally, one who gave up a beef feedlot to rabbit farm), it is through working with the land, not being a passive observer of it, that one becomes tuned into the natural world. The latter view—that it is through working with nature that one truly comes to appreciate it—introduces a concept that is important in highlighting another dimension of the relationship between agrarian lifestyle and environmental awareness—namely, pragmatism. Pragmatism is a strong feature of agrarian life, which calls into question the idealistic view that agrarian lifestyles necessarily promote environmental astuteness and concern.

My first experience of agrarian life led me to idealize the relationship between farm life and concern for the environment; however, I eventually had to come to terms with the way that pragmatic farming decisions sometimes would conflict with a more idealistic relationship with nature. As I was growing up, we generated most of our food supply for the year in the family garden. We began as preschoolers by shelling peas and gradually built up the skills to plant, tend, harvest, and process the garden produce. There was a direct connection between our labour and our well-being. Although we learned to be creative, to problem solve, and to work industriously, we were also gradually assimilated into the pragmatic logic of the farm. This assimilation involved some surprises, as we began to see discrepancies between the objectives of the farm and the attitude of unconditional respect for wild things and the natural world that was inculcated in us through the more idealistic interactions with our environment, described above. A particular image stands out for me in this regard. In our elementary school years, we would play in the tank-loads of grain as they accumulated during harvest. One of our self-appointed missions was to rescue the grasshoppers who had been entrapped in the grain during the threshing process. When we proudly reported our activity to my father, he pointed out that grasshoppers were pests and that the nobility of our rescue mission was therefore suspect. Over time, an understanding of the complexity of our relationship to the natural environment emerged from our pragmatic activities. For instance, in order to avoid spraying toxic chemicals, sometimes we would be enlisted to hand-pick potato bugs from the potato plants or to uproot a cluster of wild oats that towered above a few acres of cereal crops. Destroying what to us were unwanted species served the pragmatic goals of the farm and prevented more drastic negative impacts on the natural environment, but it still involved disrupting the natural cycles of the food web.

Pessimism

Ultimately, this growing awareness of complexity led me to see the very disruptive characteristics of agriculture. While initially I may have learned to respect nature, I also learned to justify or ignore the negative impacts of farming on the environment. In later years, I have come to comprehend the truly destructive nature of modern agriculture. For instance, I now recognize that the surplus of potato bugs in the garden resulted from the monoculture approach to gardening that we adopted and, therefore, that the killing of these bugs was not just a chance evil but one of our own making. We created the conditions for species over-population and then had to resort to crushing or drowning the creatures who took advantage of the niche we had created for them. Since humans are heterotrophs (dependent upon external sources of energy), producing food for humans isn't wrong; however, the way we have chosen to do it has contributed to massive environmental damage and impeded our ability to develop a positive relationship with nature.

My consciousness of the relationship between agriculture and the environment has changed over time, but so too has the way farming is done. I remember vividly the day that a huge green Co-op Implements self-propelled combine was delivered to our property. It was the first big piece of equipment we received on the farm. It was also, in a way, a sign of things to come. Compared to the pull-type machines without cabs that my father had used, this was a luxury model. It improved his working conditions dramatically. It had a climate-controlled cab that kept out the dust and shaded him from the sun. It was much bigger and could take in a wider swathe, which made harvesting faster. For my father this represented a change that made his life more comfortable—he did not need to work the extremely long hours he had been accustomed to and he did not work in such gruelling and hazardous conditions—exposed to noise, dust, intense sun, and rain. At the community level, however, the use of larger equipment led to catastrophic changes—a reality that did not escape my father's analysis. As equipment got more sophisticated and bigger, land holdings grew. More land was required to make a living at farming and fewer new farmers could afford to begin an operation. Over time, fewer farmers began to farm larger areas, goods and services were acquired at larger service centres, and rural communities began to shrink and disintegrate.

This disintegration of small rural communities is evident in the dramatic transformations that occurred in my lifetime in the farm community in which I grew up. At the time of my birth, the hamlet we lived in had three grain elevators, a post office, a gas station and convenience store, a one-room schoolhouse, a rail station, a church, a general store, and up to ten resident families. Today it has not one of these services, and perhaps two resident families. The school shut its doors before I was old enough to attend, and I was taken by bus fifteen miles away on a forty-five-minute trip to a multi-classroom elementary school, then later to the high school in a town twenty miles away. The elevators were eliminated one by one and eventually replaced by a more distant inland terminal to which grain is trucked rather than shipped by rail. Local postal service was lost in the late seventies. Gradually the other businesses became non-viable and closed, never to be replaced. The highway sign for Lorlie still exists, but marks something less than a ghost town. All these transitions were tied to changes in agriculture that led to rural depopulation and centralization.

The same economic forces that led to expansion of average farm size also increased mechanization and encouraged cash cropping for export. These forces in turn spawned two more drastic changes—the development of chemical controls for weeds and pests and the combining of genetic material from naturally incompatible species. Both changes are controlled and promoted by large corporations and have proceeded despite incomplete awareness of the inherent risks. I know from first-hand experience that as pesticide and herbicide use intensified, there was initially very little awareness of the hazards posed by such chemicals. One summer my brother and I stood as markers in the field so that my father would know where he had sprayed. As he completed each pass, we would run to the edge of the sprayed area, so he could line up the booms for the next pass. Another time I was hired to hand-paint the wooden floor of the grain truck with the pesticide malathion—an activity I completed clad in shorts and a tank top. I recall such incidents with the same kind of horror I experience now walking to work past city lawns redolent with toxins. And, along with many sceptical consumers, I wonder what atrocities we are unwittingly unleashing through our new-found skill of genetic manipulation.

The pace at which change has taken place in western agriculture is phenomenal. When my grandfather farmed, mixed farming was commonplace, horses were the principal energy source, manure was used as fertilizer, and chemicals for weed and pest control were unimagined. In my father's lifetime, the emphasis shifted away from mixed farming to cereal crop production, then gradually expanded to include oilseeds and pulses; there was a complete transition towards mechanization and fossil-fuel dependence; and pesticide and herbicide use became commonplace. As my brother takes over, the varieties of crops grown have further expanded, genetically modified seeds are touted as the solution for worldwide starvation, chemical use has superseded tilling as the means of weed control, and remote-operated computerized systems for farming are becoming technologically feasible. The pace of change is so rapid that there has been insufficient time to carefully consider the implications of any one of these changes, not to mention their combined effects.

If the pace of change in western agriculture has proceeded at breakneck pace, it has not taken place in the absence of some critical commentary. In Aldo Leopold's time, long before he could have known the extent of the changes that would take place in rural life, he was warning of the perils of widespread ignorance about the land:

> Perhaps the most serious obstacle impeding the evolution of a land ethic is the fact that our educational and economic system is headed away from, rather than toward, an intense consciousness of land. Your true modern is separated from the land by many middlemen, and by innumerable physical gadgets. He has no vital relation to it; to him it is the space between cities on which crops grow. Turn him loose for a day on the land, and if the spot does not happen to be a golf links or a "scenic" area, he is bored stiff.... In short, land is something he has outgrown. (1968, 223–24)

In Western countries, alienation from the land has intensified as the number of farmers has drastically decreased (only two or three percent of the

Canadian population are now farmers and, of those, most require off-farm income to survive economically). In addition, as technology "advances," those who continue to farm become more and more distanced from the soil in which their crops grow. Agrarian life, which was once a powerful means of forging relations with the natural world, has been all but lost as a positive environmental force. Can it be replaced with means of food production that will meet human needs, while avoiding substantial environmental harm, and reconnect humans positively to nature?

Idealistic Pragmatism

Permaculture (or permanent agriculture) is an approach to agriculture that has the potential to combine the best elements of agriculture—namely, its idealistic potential to create bonds between humans and nature and its pragmatic ability to supply humans with food energy. The permaculture philosophy is that it is possible to establish permanent agriculture appropriate to the characteristics of almost any region (including urban settings, where such places as balconies, building walls, and rooftops are used to grow food). The aim ought to be achieved by observing, emulating, and, finally, improving upon natural systems to maximize their benefits to humans while maintaining ecological integrity. Rather than primarily growing annuals, native varieties of perennials are established and left to grow with relatively little maintenance. Since permaculture addresses agriculture and culture, housing is also designed to be consistent with natural features and can be creatively constructed to work with nature to fashion comfortable yet functional homes (for example, building into cliff faces in order to provide natural insulation). Passive solar technologies and natural systems for climate control are used in individual buildings. However, the approach can be applied on any scale—from modifying or constructing individual homes and yards to creating whole communities. At the community level, permaculture design leads to almost self-sustaining settlements, with such features as channels for water collection that eliminate the need for irrigation yet produce lush, permanent vegetation that supplies food, shelter, and cooling effects to areas that normally require year-round air conditioning and irrigation. The ideas of working with nature and letting nature do much of the work are integral to the philosophy of permaculture.

Because permaculture can be applied in any place, and intends to make full use of existing, underused urban spaces for food production, it has the potential to reconnect people directly to the land. It should lead to more people having meaningful connections with place through providing their own food. It aims to be pragmatic but not exploitative—that is, to provide humans with food resources while requiring minimal labour and causing minimal disruption to the natural environment. In this sense it fits closely with the spirit of Rowe's ecological ethic. He says, "To imitate Nature, to join her and be bound to her rather than seeking always to transform her, is the goal that could rescue the race from barbarism and darkness" (1990, 77–78). Rowe is clear that humans are creatures of value, but recognizes that our lives are dependent upon the ecosphere. Thus, caring for ourselves necessarily involves caring for the wider ecosystem. In his words, "All organisms necessarily live by and from the Ecosphere. Valuing the planetary environment for itself neither means its non-use nor proscribes every form of 'pollution,' if that means the release of unhealthy wastes. It *does* mean directing resource use in conserving rather than exploitive ways, maintaining genetic diversity and essential ecosystem processes" (1990, 121).

Permaculture is based on these same principles. It is predicated on understanding and protecting the integrity of the global ecosystem, yet it advocates adapting portions of the ecosphere for the satisfaction of human needs using nature as a guide. Harvesting from nature should not disrupt the integrity of the adapted system. Genetic diversity will be maximized, as the objective of permaculture is to create a complex, self-sustaining system using as many varieties of native plants and animals as possible rather than growing large areas of concentrated monocultures. Thus, permaculture is one approach to agriculture that contains the seeds of sustainability. It holds promise as a means to reconnect a large proportion of people to nature while providing high-quality food for humans without unduly disrupting the natural ecosystem.

Conclusion

I lament my own distance from the agrarian life I once lived, but even more profound is my sadness when I think that my daughters will not grow up with the same connection to place or appreciation for nature as I did. Now their world is filled largely with plastic toys, stuffed animals, and shopping malls. This reality is represented in one corner of my brain by the haunting image of a miniature eighteen-month-old sobbing uncontrollably, unable to comprehend our inability to enter the mall while walking late one wintery night. Juxtaposed against this image is one of a raspberry-red smile of delight gleaned from fruit plucked fresh from the cane in our backyard by my daughters. This latter image allows me to imagine a future for my daughters in which they know where and how food is grown, they are intimate with nature, and they have a humble appreciation for their place in the wider ecosystem. Growing food in our backyard is one step toward developing in my daughters an agrarian consciousness. Probably my family and I will never return permanently to my prairie roots; nonetheless, I hope we will be among many who go forward to craft home places where food grows in abundance, the ecosystem is crawling with complexity, housing design connects us benignly with the earth, and communion with nature is a daily ritual. To preserve, better yet, enhance and pass on to another generation these legacies of agrarian life would help us to recover one historically important avenue for raising environmental consciousness or of growing roots in nature.

Note

1   To be true to Butala's writing, it must be noted that she makes a very clear distinction between farm life and ranch life, maintaining that farm life does not involve as close and sustained a connection with the natural world as ranching (1994, 33).

Works Cited

Baltaz, Diane P. *Living Off the Land: A Spirituality of Farming*. Ottawa: Novalis, 1991.

Butala, Sharon. *The Perfection of the Morning: An Apprenticeship in Nature*. Toronto: HarperCollins, 1994.

Laurence, Margaret. "Via Rail and Memory." In *Dance on the Earth: A Memoir*. Toronto: McClelland & Stewart, 1989.

Leopold, Aldo. *A Sand County Almanac and Sketches Here and There*. London: Oxford University Press, 1968.

O'Sullivan, Edmund. *Transformative Learning: Educational Vision for the 21st Century*. New York: Zed, 1999.

Rowe, Stan. *Home Place: Essays on Ecology*. Edmonton: NeWest, 1990.

4

The Marginal World
Catriona Mortimer-Sandilands

I

> The edge of the sea is a strange and beautiful place. All through
> the long history of Earth it has been an area of unrest where
> waves have broken heavily against the land, where the tides
> have pressed forward over the continents, receded, and
> then returned. For no two successive days is the
> shore line precisely the same.
> —*Rachel Carson*

On a bright August afternoon near the end of our annual Victoria holiday, my daughter Hannah and I returned to the beach at Cadboro Bay equipped with the accoutrements of a (then) two-year-old's minor adventure: obligatory sunscreen and hat, towels, purple shovel, yellow pail, trucks, net, and jar. The air was rich with children's happy shouting and Hannah joined right in, barely waiting until I had helped her off with her shirt to sprint down to the edge of the sand, shrieking with delight at the cold salt sea that crept over her toes. However much the beach had changed—the one I remembered from my own childhood seemed larger, wilder, less pinkly suburban—this joy of rushing down from hot sand to cold ocean had not. I followed my daughter, adding my own loud pleasure to the mix.

Later, on one of our trips from water's edge to in-progress sandcastle with our pail of seaweedy water, Hannah stopped at the line of greenish foam that marked the afternoon's high tide. A small transparent bubble had caught her eye, and she crouched down to look at it more closely. It did nothing. She poked it. It didn't break or do anything one might expect of a bubble; it wobbled slightly. As my daughter grinned at this wonderful novelty of a shining, beached jellyfish (dead), I remembered other discoveries in this rich, wet borderland: elephant kelp whips, rare whole sand dollars, tiny bullheads to be caught and released, log-boom escapees for sea-going voyages, once a dead seal carcass with its eyes already eaten, the reality of washed-up bleach bottles beckoning to the promise of prized Japanese fishing floats, and, much later, the eroticism of the movement between moon and water.

I was privileged, I think, to have grown up in this place, at the (then) edge of a city on the edge of an island on the edge of a country. (This in addition to the other privileges of my birth: white, middle-class, only child.) Quite apart from the climate and physical beauty that have made Victoria one of the fastest-growing real estate markets in Canada (hence the increased suburban presence on Cadboro Bay), I think the beach helped to give me an appreciation of margins, liminal zones, transitional spaces, borderlands (and this, perhaps, despite my other privileges). I like seashores, foothills, wetlands, estuaries. I like train stations, foyers, atriums, theatres. I also like equinoxes, the tickling cool of fall in the heat of summer, the first snowdrops in January (Victoria) or April (Ontario). I like in-between spaces, transition times in which two realms collide, in which the collective life of one intermingles with and disrupts another, bringing something new into being. I like unlikely combinations and take enormous pleasure in putting together things that don't normally belong. (So does Hannah, so I have to relearn that it really doesn't hurt to put ketchup in your yogurt.) I like places and times that are pregnant with change.

Florence Krall calls these edge-zones "ecotones." Biologically, ecotones are transitional regions between two different habitats. Rife with the species of both areas, ecotones are places of diversity, combination, novelty, adaptation. "To an ecologist," writes Krall, "the 'edge effect' carries the connotation of a complex interplay of life forces where plant communities, and the creatures they support, intermingle in mosaics or change abruptly." But also metaphorically: "much like the ecotones in biotic communities, [margins in social and cultural contexts] may be rich and dynamic transitional zones and may provide great learning as well as suffering" (1994, 4). The places where cultures, natures, life worlds, experiences, and ideas collide and intermingle are ecotones; the places on the margins where mainstream culture is met and challenged by other forms are particularly fertile with possibilities for change.

II

> The interaction between human-constructed and
> natural environments can no longer be ignored;
> culture and ecology are interactive.
> —*Florence Krall*

Environmental studies, my chosen field of work, is centrally concerned with the interfaces between human and biotic (or, if you prefer, human and non-human) communities. For most people, the term probably evokes things like monitoring ozone depletion, protecting wilderness preserves, managing water quality, reducing pollution, negotiating acid rain agreements: the measurement and mitigation of human impacts on nature. To be sure, that's all part of it, but for me environmental studies is really about natural-cultural ecotones: the understanding of human-nonhuman mutuality, conflict, change, influence. These relationships comprise much more than the biophysical impact of one on the other; they concern the ways in which human lives are inextricably and variously intermingled with the lives of the animate creatures and inanimate objects with which we share time and space. Because these relationships are complex, environmental studies cannot possibly rely on ecological science alone to understand them; because these relationships are social and cultural as well as biological and physical, good environmental studies needs sociology, history, and literary criticism as much as it does zoology, botany, and geology.

Crucially, environmental studies is about unravelling and understanding what Alexander Wilson called "cultures of nature." For Wilson, "our experience of the natural world—whether touring the Canadian Rockies, watching an animal show on TV, or working in our own gardens—is always mediated," always encultured (1991, 12). Even when we are apparently alone in the wilderness, we bring with us in our mental daypacks the contradictory ideas and practices of nature in which we cannot help but be immersed by virtue of being alive in the social world; nature "is always shaped by rhetorical constructs like photography, industry, advertising and aesthetics, as well as by institutions like religion, tourism and education" (1991, 12). This shaping does not occur only inside human minds. Ideas of nature intervene in the ways we construct and organize nature itself. Such interventions range from building scenic highways and nature park facilities to foster particular sweeping views of trees, mountains, or grand stretches of water; to the attempt at complete banishment of microbial nature from most Western, middle-class households at the hands of a new generation of "anti-bacterial" soaps, cleansers, and assorted other chemicals; to heated debates about whether or not to slaughter Canada geese who are perceived as over-populous, disease-bearing, urban nuisances at the same time as they stand as iconic representatives of the true north strong and free. Our cultures of nature are multiple, contradictory, embodied, historical, and, in many cases, highly controversial. They are, like the edge of the sea, shifting terrains where two complex systems meet, embrace, clash, and transform one another.

Of course, this means that environmental studies, as a border-practice straddling culture and nature, isn't just about human ideas and practices. Nature may be caught up in and shaped by tides of social and cultural action, but that doesn't mean that humans are the only actors. "In fact," wrote Wilson, "the whole idea of nature as something separate from human experience is a lie. Humans and nature construct one another" (1991, 13). As soon as one is willing to think of human-nonhuman interaction as an ecotone, a zone of contest, change, and co-construction, a door is opened to a fantastic range of cross-species, cross-disciplinary, and cross-cultural conversations.

III

> Some human-made boundaries are recognized and used by
> wild animals. For example, the Waterton elk herd knows the east
> boundary of the park very well. In the summer, it will range in
> and out of the park in search of plentiful green grasses. But
> in the fall, when the grass has turned brown and hunting
> season opens outside the park, it grazes within the
> park boundary where no hunters wait in ambush.
> —*Don H. Meredith*

The Prince of Wales Hotel in Waterton Lakes National Park is pompous, overpriced, kitschy, and a bit shabby beyond the cavernous, tartan-decorated and oil-painting-laden lobby. But it is located at one of my favourite places in the world. Unlike much of the eastern slope of the Alberta Rockies, there are no real foothills in Waterton (it's a geological thing). So if you look west, the Rocky Mountains are immediately before you, reflected in Upper Waterton Lake and stretching up from there with snow-tipped fingers thousands of metres into the sky; turn around 180 degrees and there are the prairies, stretched out, gentle, gold-green, and horizontal to the limit of possible vision. And if you look down (well, if you look down somewhere other than the lawn of the Prince of Wales), you see alpine and prairie wildflowers mingled in a colourful, and what I anthropomorphize as exuberant and joyful, coexistence: alumroot, beargrass, saxifrage, arnica, columbine, penstemon, larkspur, both mountain and meadow death camas.

Waterton is an ecotone, a margin, and "where the mountains meet the prairie" is part of its official Parks Canada theme. In its existence as part of the Waterton-Glacier International Peace Park, which straddles the border between Alberta and Montana, it is also part of a cultural margin within and between two nations, a negotiated mingling of Canadian and American ideas of nature, nation, and culture. In this (literal) borderland, different park policies, different policing powers, different management priorities, different styles of recreation, different sensibilities around rights and space and aesthetics and freedom collide and intermingle as everything from bears to tourists to invasive plant spores to smugglers travel from the one side of the forty-ninth parallel to the other. The border itself is marked by a cleared swath that, interestingly, is more remarkable for its own complete irrelevance than anything else; as one Parks Canada interpreter put it, if it weren't there then we couldn't talk about the fact that it shouldn't be. It's not that there aren't differences between the two parks or nations, only that they are far more complex than a line transecting the landscape into "here" and "there" can represent. For one thing, as is the case with so many Canada–US transitions, it's only the Canadians who seem to care that there may be a change at all.

National parks have, historically, tended to rely on a clear demarcation of borders in order to enforce preservation of wildlife and habitats "inside" against the threats posed by extractive industries, agriculture, and even residential development "outside." Waterton, however, is an irony. It relies on the fact that it is adjacent, on its prairie side, to "habitat ranchers outside the park have protected for more than a century. Its wildlife abundance is at least as much the result of cattle ranching as it is of park protection" (Van Tighem 2000, 172). Inside Waterton, park conservation staff struggle with the invasive ornamental plant species that cottagers and hoteliers desire as part of their recreational nature aesthetic, and with some locals' desires for a greater tourist presence in the grand style of Jasper and Banff (the Prince of Wales doesn't quite compare—yet). Outside Waterton, ranchers who have been so frequently vilified for killing large carnivores (that is, the ones that attack cattle) are now charged with the task of protecting the biological diversity, on which precisely these large carnivores (and others) depend, against a growing sea of semi-commuters who are drawn to the remarkable beauty of the region and to the increasingly accessible park.

Irony, it seems, is also a feature of ecotones; interstitial spaces allow interesting becomings.

IV

> *To live in the Borderlands means you*
> *are neither* hispana India negra espaòñla
> ni gabacha, eres mestiza, mulata, *half-breed*
> *caught in the crossfire between camps*
> *while carrying all five races on your back*
> *not knowing which side to turn to, run from.*
> —Gloria Anzaldúa

As Krall notes, margins are simultaneously places of potentially rich intermingling and, in the context of historical and contemporary power relations, sites of staggering inequality and oppression. "The ecotone, which, in the natural world provides a dynamic interchange, becomes exceedingly complex as a cultural metaphor and may represent a barrier that blocks some people from their rightful place in the scheme of things" (1994, 5). Surely then, it is partly because I am able to inhabit so many apparent centres—class, race, nation—that I am able to *desire* the risks and uncertainties of the borderlands, to *choose* elements of a critical distance afforded by an edge. And surely also, I am complicit in the ways the contemporary world organizes its centres and margins, responsible for interrogating and challenging these power relations.

But it is not only that. I move to the edge zones because they also remind me that we are all, in some respects, marginal creatures: in process from one state to another, mixtures, amalgams, hybrids, mutants. Gloria Anzaldúa's writing shows the power of hybridity, what she calls *mestiza* consciousness, for her a mixture of birth circumstance and active political cultivation. Her embodied border-crossings of race, gender, nation, and sexuality do not allow her to settle complacently into a single, comfortable place or identity. Rather, they propel and enable her to see the world partially and multiply, to understand contradiction and paradox, to see both pain and pleasure in intermingling, and to create poetry in the new possibilities wrought by collision, rather than mourn for a lost purity or simplicity.

Indeed, for Donna Haraway this world of hybridity and boundary-crossing is not just about shifts in cultural identity produced by conquest and diasporic migration, but is also fundamentally concerned with the ongoing transgression of human bodily boundaries—and other apparently organic wholes—in a cyborg world. Certainly, there is ample reason to struggle against a techno-scientific world that genetically combines pig with tomato, computer chip with human brain, in a vast imposition of capitalist control on human and non-human natures. But

> from another perspective, a cyborg world might be about lived social and bodily realities in which people are not afraid of their joint kinship with animals and machines, not afraid of permanently partial identities and contradictory standpoints. The political struggle is to see from both perspectives at once because each reveals both dominations and possibilities unimaginable from the other vantage point. (1991, 154)

Recognizing ourselves as ecotones, as rich mixtures of culture, nature, animal, and technology, may allow us to think critically about our human lives in our biotic and technological communities without resorting to nostalgic fantasies about innocence, purity, a fall from grace. The critical question, then, is not about erecting and maintaining boundaries of safety around a carefully cherished utopia, but about investigating and challenging the multiple threads of power that twist intricately in our interactions with non-human natures, that shape our cultural and biological minds and bodies, that organize and reorganize the worlds of the non-human creatures with whom we interact.

V

In this difficult world of the shore, life displays its enormous
toughness and vitality by occupying almost every conceivable niche.
Visibly, it carpets the intertidal rocks; or half hidden, it descends
into fissures and crevices, or hides under boulders, or lurks in the
wet gloom of sea caves. Invisibly, where the casual observer
would say there is no life, it lies deep in the sand, in
burrows and tubes and passageways.
—*Rachel Carson*

Hannah and I looked at the jellyfish for a while, and then began to notice that its body was really part of a small and lively dance. Around it, tiny organisms were beginning to nibble its fringes. Nearby, a small pile of kelp afforded temporary shelter for a minute and frantic crab. A few brine shrimp hopped anarchically away from the retreating tide. A hopeful seagull padded closer, not quite sure if we were a source of or a barrier to food. Emergence, retreat, approach, flight: the shore contained a constant interaction, of which we were, at that moment, a conscious part. But such direct consciousness is often fragile; my two-year-old naturalist's attention span came to its limit, so we went back to our sand pile. There, the pail of water helped us transform the dry sand into a magnificent birthday cake, which we garnished with driftwood candles, feathers, and broken seashells, artifacts of the sea and traces of our encounter becoming architectural features of our imagination.

The jellyfish will jumble up in Hannah's memory with the crabs, the seagull, the ocean, the cake, and the afternoon's promised popsicle. Who knows what footprints it will eventually leave, what consciousness it will inspire in her, how this edge will figure in our developing relationship? Who knows what the dead jellyfish said to her or what language the movement of the tides will allow her to hear in the future? Edges bear considerable responsibility; they are places where we encounter the Other, where we see and hear, if we look and listen closely, lives and languages that are different from our own, where we feel, if we think with our skins, the press of other bodies impacting us. Mingled-up sites of the banal and the wondrous, ecotones are zones of meeting, impact, crossing. Their diversity affords us chances to touch and be touched by a range of other lives that far exceeds a single culture, a single species. The greater the diversity that margins foster—cultural, biological, or both—the richer and more complex our interactions with the Other.

The linkage of biological and cultural diversity is problematic on some counts (I get especially nervous when sociobiologists claim that cultural diversity and like social phenomena are essentially bio-evolutionary qualities, a claim that does considerable violence to the complexities of both human and other animal cultures), but it can serve as a useful metaphor in developing a political or ethical response to eco-cultural issues. Think of it this way: the destruction of nature, say, by clear-cutting a forest may be ecologically bad, but it is also culturally harmful, as elements of a local life world are removed from possibility, as threads of a culture of nature wither and die. One doesn't only lose trees and moss; one loses a complex array of human interactions with them, ranging from stories, maps, and metaphors to food, medicine, and building materials. Conversely, globalizing commodity fetishism—the profound reduction of multiple cultures of creation and use to a single practice of exchange—also impoverishes nature. As First Peoples, for example, lose their historical hunting, gathering, and ceremonial practices to a singular narrative of buying and selling (including, in many cases, tourism), nature becomes an exploitable object of exchange, a scarce resource, a set of rights, a spectacle, rather than an animate realm of acting and creative beings with whom one interacts as an Other among others.

I am not advocating a nostalgic return to some pre-capitalist culture of nature, nor am I suggesting that only subsistence activities or wilderness experiences bring one "close" to nature. I don't understand all contemporary culture as a loss or death of nature, and I think there are many places in which new and diverse cultures of nature are coming into being (some, but not all of which are brought about by environmentalism). Indeed, I hope that I am clear that I see the richness of the margins in everyday life, that ecotones can include the suburban natures of local beaches, and that ecology crucially involves developing relationships to the contemporary coexistence of *multiple* cultures of nature, not just a more singular one that would focus on parks, wilderness, or preservation (indeed, preservationism does not necessarily challenge homogenization, but that is another story). But there is a tension between living the richness of the everyday and recognizing and challenging the ways in which contemporary, destructive power relations shape the current world of culture-nature interaction. This tension propels us to speak about environmental justice, cultural survival, democratic access to environmental decision making, economic diversification, and so-called alternative forms of cultural creativity as foundational elements of environmental politics, not just as add-ons to a primary goal of biodiversity protection. This tension requires that we understand nature is not a separable realm to be managed apart from human life, that the protection and creation of cultural diversity helps to promote the protection and creation of biodiversity (and vice versa), and that the margins of the two realms are vital to both.

For me, then, environmental politics is about protecting the possibility of the edge, the margin, the ecotone, which crucially includes *cultivating* the multiple and fertile eco-cultural crescents along which nature seeps into our consciousness, our representations, our political demands. To paraphrase Haraway, this kind of eco-cultural politics is thus about taking *pleasure* in the edges and also *responsibility* for their construction. This kind of action moves us always away from comfortable centres, including mainstream cultures of nature. It takes us to the borders, where things may get messy, risky, and unpredictable, but where new awareness and new life may emerge from encounters with difference. After all, if we spend too long in the centre, we may lose our edge altogether.

Works Cited

Anzaldúa, Gloria. *Borderlands/La Frontera: The New Mestiza*. San Francisco: Spinsters/Aunt Lutte, 1987.

Carson, Rachel. *The Edge of the Sea*. New York: Houghton Mifflin, 1955.

Haraway, Donna. *Simians, Cyborgs and Women: The Reinvention of Nature*. New York: Routledge, 1991.

Krall, Florence. *Ecotone: Wayfaring on the Margins*. Albany: State University of New York Press, 1994.

Meredith, Don H. "On Borders and Boundaries." In *Voices in the Wind: A Waterton-Glacier Anthology*, ed. Barbara Grinder, Valerie Haig-Brown, and Kevin Van Tighem. Waterton Park, AB: Waterton Natural History Association, 2000.

Van Tighem, Kevin. "Hope on the Range." In *Voices in the Wind: A Waterton-Glacier Anthology*, op. cit.

Wilson, Alexander. *The Culture of Nature: North American Landscape from Disney to the Exxon Valdez*. Toronto: Between the Lines, 1991.

5

Reflections of a Zealot

Elizabeth May

My life in the environmental movement is not something I entirely understand. It is certainly not a "career" in any traditional sense. Unlike a career path, it's not something over which I feel I've had any intention or will. It is like being born female. I was born an environmentalist, although I was probably trained as an activist. Equal parts nature and nurture.

It is beyond me to know how or why I felt connected to the natural world from my earliest awareness. My mother told me, and anyone else who would listen, that as a small child I told her I didn't like airplanes because they scratched the sky. I do remember loving all the tiny flowers no one else could see. And I can still recall the feel of the bark on my most favourite trees around my childhood home—a smooth, papery birch, amazing, flaky bark from the giant sycamore. My father built a tree house for my brother and me in a wonderful gnarled old willow. Its branches formed the most fabulous space to cradle our little home, complete with its make-believe fireplace and little tea set. Like most activists I have often been asked about early stirrings of an environmental consciousness; I loved animals, particularly baby animals, as a child. (The exception was and is snakes, for which I have an embarrassingly irrational phobia.)

No doubt the seeds of my activism were sown by my mother. She was a crusader from my earliest days, campaigning against the atmospheric testing of nuclear weapons. Although the campaign is usually characterized as part of the peace movement, it had all the hallmarks of environmental concerns. Nuclear testing was distributing tons of toxic radionuclides, including strontium-90, all around the world. Strontium-90's characteristics are to mimic calcium. Taken up in grasses, consumed by dairy cows, the radiation made its way to milk. Once consumed, it was stored in bones and teeth, increasing the risk of childhood leukemia and, later, adult cancers. When other children were playing in the snow in our kindergarten, I was busy warning them not to eat the snow because of the strontium-90. I knew what it was called, I knew it was fallout from bombs, and I knew it could kill us later on.

The United States Nuclear Regulatory Commission, in Orwellian language of reassurance, labelled the amount of strontium-90 in milk as "Sunshine Units." How my mother, with no previous science background, realized that little doses of sunshine from the inside were a threat to health I don't really know. But she spent hours on the telephone tracking down scientists and doctors who were concerned about the extensive contamination of the biosphere. She ground up calcium tablets and forced us to eat the chalkiest ice cream, hoping, on the advice of one professor, to so saturate our growing bodies with real calcium that they would reject the radioactive imposter. We drank powdered milk rather than fresh in hope that the radiation had dissipated in the manufacturing process. But for my mother, precautionary steps to reduce her children's exposure were just the beginning. When I was a toddler, my mother organized against nuclear weapons testing. She and my father formed the "Connecticut Committee for a Sane Nuclear Policy." They were the whole committee when my mother started at the beginning of the Yellow Pages listing for "Clergy." She phoned every one, asking each to accept a petition to stop the distribution of nuclear fallout. When I could hardly talk, I played with a toy phone. "I want to speak to ministers, priests, and rabbis," I would say. "I have a 'tition."

In the late 1950s, my mother was part of the first truly global grassroots movement. Many of the groups were established by mothers concerned about nuclear weapons testing and the threat to their children. By the time I was six, I stood next to my mother on the plinth of Trafalgar Square at the culmination of the fifty-four-mile march to London from the military research base in Aldermaston. (I had walked on only the last two days of the trek. My mum, with air mattress and sleeping bag, had made the whole walk while my dad kept us with his parents outside London.) In that spring of 1960, 100,000 people gathered in Trafalgar Square and my mother spoke on behalf of the movement in the United States.

When I was in first grade, quite mysteriously from our teachers' viewpoint, my mother took my brother and me out of school for an unspecified amount of time. She was embarrassed to admit that she was planning to go on a hunger strike in front of the Soviet Mission to the United Nations to protest the planned atmospheric detonation of a 100-megaton bomb by the USSR. Tired of being labelled a Soviet sympathizer for her ban the bomb campaigning, not to mention tired of the anonymous threatening phone calls and hate mail, she decided to make it clear that the movement opposed any and all nuclear weapons testing, whether American or Russian or British. My brother and I stayed with friends outside New York, as my dad worked and no one in those days thought dads had much to do with looking after children. (Nevertheless, no one could have imagined a more supportive husband and father in all the years of my mother's and then my own crusades.) My mother stayed by herself in an awful hotel that evicted her. Every day she would go to the front of the Soviet mission with a sign made by a friend that allowed her to slip in a new number for the number of days of her hunger strike. By the time she had been on the hunger strike for four days, she was being interviewed by all the major newspapers and television networks, including *News of the World*, CBS, NBC, and BBC. We watched from our snug little home away from home. We had never seen our mother flickering black and white from the TV. On day six, my father went down to Manhattan to see if she wasn't ready to come home. When she got to our friends' house, I asked her, "Why have you abandoned your post?" Whether the question was bred of commitment to the cause or a reluctance to go home and back to school I really don't know, but I suspect the latter.

The grassroots political movement was rewarded when, in September 1963, the governments of the United States, Soviet Union, and United Kingdom entered into the Nuclear Test Ban Treaty. The treaty banned the testing by detonation of nuclear weapons into the atmosphere.

Thus, from my earliest years, I had no doubt that a single activist could change the world. From my point of view, it was even simpler: My mummy had made President Kennedy stop the fallout.

Little wonder, then, that the ethic of active political participation was part of the fabric of my personality. My mother had been similarly inculcated in activism by her mother, who told her frequently, "Thought without constructive action is demoralizing." It has become the family motto. We are not demoralized.

I probably would have pursued the same issues as my mother, since I was always going with her to anti-war meetings and rallies, and planning the campaigns of candidates who promised to end the conflict in Vietnam. But in the late 1960s, my love of animals brought me into the environmental movement. We had lots of animals on a seven-acre hobby farm. I grew up with ponies, sheep, chickens, an occasional donkey, and a multitude of dogs and cats.

The sheep, a small flock of six, were pets, with the birth of the lambs not only a highlight of my life but a very successful grade six science project. I bottle-fed one of the lambs, born to a ewe with zero maternal instincts. The lamb was named Corey in honour of Wrong-Way Corrigan, the famed pilot with a faulty sense of direction. Corey compounded his mother's lack of interest in raising him by searching for milk in all the wrong places, generally burrowing his head into her chest. Wrestling with mother and son to get teat to mouth never resulted in either of them figuring out how to nurse. Fortunately, we had another ewe who was a wonderful mother, easily managing the feeding of twins. The twins were the joy of our lives, leaping and clicking heels, playfully butting and frolicking all the day long. When first their mother and then one of the twins died horrible deaths, twitching and jerking in the same way as the sheep exposed to nerve gas, I kept searching for answers. The vet did an autopsy, looking for any signs of poisonous plants or berries in stomach contents. No explanation for their deaths could be found. Years passed until in grade nine I read Rachel Carson's *Silent Spring*. In it I recognized the symptoms of the deaths attributed to chlorinated hydrocarbon pesticides. I wrote the municipal government and asked if any spraying had been done in our area around the time our sheep had died. Sure enough, they had sprayed with the organophosphate insecticides methoxychlor and malathion. Suddenly I became more aware of all pesticide use. I asked my mother about the DDT spraying against mosquitoes. When I was a child, we had welcomed the fog of DDT as it wafted across our lawn. In spite of her opposition to atmospheric fallout, my mother had had no qualms about the wonders of DDT. Babies were safer with DDT around, killing those nasty mosquitoes.

I found my first personal "cause" as a pesticide activist. But it quickly led to others. In 1970 I organized for the first Earth Day. By high school, I had converted a piece of Oregon returnable-bottle legislation and had it introduced to the Connecticut legislature (it passed after my family had moved to Cape Breton). I organized a high-school campaign to get phosphates out of laundry detergents, which was a remarkably successful win, coming as it did when national concern about eutrophication[1] was at its height. High-school environmental clubs were springing up all over. Working with new friends in the Hartford area, we organized the Environmental Action Regional Taskforce of Hartford (EARTH), a coalition of thirty-five different high-school environmental groups. EARTH took on a challenge from Ralph Nader to raise funds to open the first of what would become the Public Interest Research Groups. For Earth Day in 1971, we held a walk-a-thon and a concert with Pete Seeger, raising $35,000, which was matched by Nader to get the Connecticut Citizens' Action Group off the ground.

By then I was certain of my academic and professional life. I wanted to be an environmental lawyer; I wanted to go to Yale Law School, accelerate my undergraduate degree, and finish law school in 1978; I wanted to move to Washington, DC, and sue polluters for one of the major environmental groups. Instead, my life took an unexpected detour.

After a vacation in Nova Scotia in 1972, my parents decided to move to Cape Breton Island. We knew only the handful of people we had met in a whimsical quest for property. We bought one hundred acres overlooking the Bras d'Or, which, after another summer, led to buying a dilapidated restaurant and gift shop on the Cabot Trail. We emigrated: my whole family, three dogs, two cats, two ponies, and an elderly Corey, the sole survivor of our little flock. Instead of starting law school, I embarked on a new career—cooking and waitressing.

Thoughts of a law practice avenging ravaged Mother Earth disappeared in a haze of fish and chips. Certainly I had never lived such an isolated or impoverished existence. My family's investment in renovating the gift shop and restaurant was met with a sea of red ink. I also had never lived anywhere so beautiful, with miles of breathtaking coastline. Despite an American childhood, I had never seen the "national bird," the bald eagle, until our first summer in Cape Breton. I became an instant addict. Cape Breton's landscapes had captured my heart. What's more, my family was too broke to think of sending me to finish university. I had no expectation of ever doing anything other than running the restaurant.

At the time of our move, I worried that I was abandoning my activism. Like most Americans, I thought that the only important events in the world happened within the US. I felt I was surrendering my commitment to environmental work as my brother and I followed our parents to the edge of nowhere, a village of forty-some people on the southern coast of the Gulf of St. Lawrence. I needn't have worried. Within three years of our big move, I was at the centre of a major grassroots uprising to prevent aerial insecticide spraying.

In the fall of 1975, the Nova Scotia government issued a permit to spray Cape Breton's forests against the spruce budworm. Soon a petition was cranked out in the church basement in Inverness and started circulating throughout the island. It was early winter and our restaurant was closed for the season. Having signed the petition at a health food store in Sydney, I went home and dug through my old boxes for my high-school pesticide files. In the dark days before the Internet, with only the Baddeck public library available to help with research, my box of books was the best source for hundreds of miles. I rediscovered *Silent Spring*, amazed to find that Rachel Carson had dedicated a full chapter, entitled "Rivers of Death," to the devastation of New Brunswick's environment due to the budworm spray program. Between *Silent Spring* and articles from the Scientists' Institute for Public Information, I put together the first detailed fact sheet on the proposed chemical of choice—fenitrothion. An organophosphate insecticide, it was a cholinesterase inhibitor. Cholinesterase is an enzyme essential to the transmission of nerve impulses. Spruce budworms would be killed by blocking the transmission of signals—sending their nervous systems into a flashing mess. Humans have the same enzyme that performs the same function. In other words, in a large enough dose it would kill just like the pesticides that had killed my pet lambs years ago.

From that moment on, my life in Canada became as defined by activism as had my previous existence in the US. We fought budworm spraying as an annual event. Like tourism, fighting the budworm spraying was a seasonal activity. Blessedly, these two completely consuming activities occupied different seasons. I lived a summer and fall of kitchen servitude, followed by a winter and spring of grassroots organizing. Much of the budworm campaign was financed from my waitressing tips and unemployment insurance cheques. After our group successfully protected Cape Breton from annual dousings with chemical poisons, I became involved in opposing the nuclear power plant sitting near the earthquake fault line at Point Lepreau, New Brunswick. In the spring of 1980 I learned there was a law school programme for mature students with less than perfect undergraduate credentials, and decided to apply. Slightly off my original schedule, I started Dalhousie Law School two years after I had intended to finish. The demands of volunteer activism have kept surfacing, and I haven't had as much as a one-month period over the last twenty years when I was not working on one campaign or other.

So what is my connection to the natural environment now? I live in a city, Ottawa, to be better able to work for environmental goals. I cannot see most of the stars in the night sky. There are no northern lights, and eagles do not soar and circle overhead. Still, as I take the train from Ottawa to Toronto, my most frequent route, I do see the occasional great blue heron take wing. I enjoy the walk along the Rideau River, watching its resident ducks in my most meandering walk to work. I am blessed with a treed neighbourhood, able to find deep woods for a morning walk with our dog as easily as turning in another direction to catch my downtown-bound bus. I go home to Cape Breton as much as possible and count the circling eagles as my friends, taking their appearance at important moments in campaigns as omens. My daughter inspires my activism now. Seeing the world through her eyes is a never-ending joy. But as much as having a child has made me indescribably happy, it has also intensified my rage over the selfish, short-sighted decisions which poison our bodies and tear away at our life-support system. The threats are not to some external concept of "environment." The threats are to my daughter's future.

And so, I feel the sense of life coming full circle. I have embraced my mother's activism and, like her, I am motivated now by the desire to have a liveable world in which my daughter can grow up. Environmental activism is like breathing. I won't be done until I'm done.

Note

1   Eutrophication is caused by over-fertilization of a water body, choking out life through algal blooms.

Work Cited

Carson, Rachel. *Silent Spring*. Boston: Houghton Mifflin, 1962.

6

Going Home
Memories of the Natural World

J. A. Wainwright

The Pond

In recent years I've approached it from the west, and for a variety of reasons in the late afternoon, as if the setting sun in my rearview mirror is there to emphasize the passing of the years. It's an unassuming body of water, probably no more than one hundred metres wide and twice that in length, with a swamp and creek at its far end that serve as source and breeding ground for insects, birds, and frogs. We—my early-teen friends and I—always called it Glenville Pond because Glenville was the name of the narrow dirt road beside the water, branching off from the larger gravel road that led us eastward out of Newmarket, Ontario, on summer days in the late 1950s.

We would ride our bikes through two miles of farmland and hardwoods, holding fishing rods away from revolving spokes, and carrying bathing suits, towels, and some form of lunch in canvas knapsacks across our shoulders. It always seemed farther than two miles, not only because of the road's long inclines and brief descents, but also because the distance we travelled from our home lives was important. To set off to the pond was to ride into freedom, into a day where responsibilities of school and domesticity could be forgotten, and toward a place where the echoes of delighted cries and splashes would drown out the adult demands of our coming high-school years.

The pond was at the bottom of a small valley, but despite our high-speed negotiations of rut and gravel and the resultant rush of wind that lifted our baseball caps to dry the sweat on our foreheads, we always raced to the shoreline and plunged in to wash the dust and any lingering traces of civilization from our bodies. That shoreline was a grass and mud bank only a foot or two above the water, but served, because it dropped so quickly into depths unseen, as launching pad for belly-flops and cannonballs and the occasional unstudied passage of grace from earth to air to blue-green immersion.

Once, we built a raft from several logs and boards lifted from a decaying barn in a nearby field. We nailed the boards from log to log in somewhat haphazard fashion, and launched our vessel with great fanfare, six of us piling on a bobbing platform no bigger than a dining-room table, and paddling madly with pieces of scrap. We had no way to anchor in the centre of the pond, so the raft drifted in the breeze or was propelled by our continual jumping off, individually or in group formation, and eventually we would end up by the swamp where the algae would coat the ends of the logs and glisten in our hair as we emerged, the water beading on our torsos like a cuirass. We had no masks or snorkels, but it would have made no difference if we had. The pond was thick with soil runoff, and when we opened our eyes underwater we could see the bottom of the raft and flashing limbs, but little else beyond drifting particles of plants and nutrients that were quite distinct where sunlight penetrated, but at greater depth, or when clouds closed in, became a brown wall of claustrophobic impact we would challenge one another to mark with deeper and deeper dives.

After lunch, washed down with pond water taken from the supposedly cleaner exit flow of a culvert-formed waterfall, we would lie back for awhile and take in the sky that ducks and songbirds criss-crossed in calligraphic formations we tried vaguely to decipher. We listened to their calls through a distance of daydreams that themselves could not be translated except as affirmations of unquestioned existence in a natural world we took so much for granted. The pond and trees would always be there for our pleasure, and the sun would always shine on our unlined, receptive bodies that, once naturally tanned, needed no other protection than the earth's inviolate presence in space and time.

Later on, some of us would flick our brightly shining lures through the afternoon air, surprised at the strength of the small-mouth bass who hit them, their fierce determination to survive. After the struggle, we released them in slippery confusions of scale and skin. That was our part of the bargain. If their jaws were torn or bleeding from the barbs, we pretended not to notice. Instead we watched the flick of tail fins, iridescent, as they disappeared. Their part of the bargain was that they would always return.

Now when I drive by the pond on a two-lane highway that takes Newmarket commuters to their six-lane route to Toronto, I am usually in a hurry with a destination to reach at a certain hour. But I always anticipate the gleam of light off the water and the surrounding trees, and plan ahead for my one-hundred-kilometre-per-hour glance at what seems to have remained remarkably unaffected by a world of schedule and flux. Despite the widening and paving of the road, the dimensions of the shoreline haven't changed, though the water level is not as high as it used to be, and there is an encroachment of swamp at the far end where ragged stumps rise in profusion and the meandering creek line is more visible than before. I never see any swimmers or even a solitary fisherman on the bank. The pond appears unused, except as storage basin for whatever pollutants make their way into the creek as runoff from nearby super-farms or fall directly as acid rain that initially forms above the chimneys of Pittsburgh and Cleveland, not to mention the nearby plants and refineries of southern Ontario. I'm sure that any blue-green immersions occur only in the private pools that glisten behind houses lining the highway in prosperous rows at the top of the rise. I am in the suburbs of life now. The country, like the bass and boyhood, has gone.

The Valley

I wonder sometimes whether I belong to the last generation, in the Western world at least, that can recall the different landscape of youth. Of course, things change for everyone, no matter what age, but I am speaking here of the experience of integral natural-world territories apart from housing developments, malls, and general urban sprawl. It's not only the pond I remember. In the late 1980s, after I have been living away from Toronto for some time, I return and take my two young sons to the Ontario Science Centre in the north-east part of the city. The Centre is built into the side of a steep ravine, and visitors descending to yet another display of human achievement can follow, through a slant of windows, the slope-line of growth outside. As I walk down the stairs and winding concourses, I suddenly realize I am re-entering a portion of the Don Valley where I played as a boy on weekends and holidays away from elementary school. More than to any scientific wonder, I am drawn to the variety of leaf and branch outside the sheets of glass, and to memories of cliff side adventures and of a river that carved its way through clay and rock in shallow curves of light.

The valley was huge and exhilarating to us, not least because of its many wild inhabitants. On our jaunts we met martens, foxes, rabbits, raccoons, and the occasional porcupine, not to mention smaller denizens like field-mice, voles, and squirrels. There were plenty of birds, including osprey, ducks, quail, and pheasants. We had no compasses, but marked our entrance by trees or outcroppings of rock near familiar streets above. We knew the river flowed north to south, and that the tops of the cliffs on either side were close to lampposts and picket fences. It must have been a simpler time in some respects. Our parents didn't seem to think we could come to any harm, and warned us only of possible encounters with hobos whose campsites we would come across in sheltered spots. "Don't touch anything that doesn't belong to you" and "Be polite" were the only admonitions in regard to human contact. We'd find empty beer and liquor bottles at these camps, and regale ourselves with stories of dangerous men, but we never actually came face to face with any threat in the valley. In truth, it was a pastoral experience we shared with each other, a harmonious sojourn into a natural world that fed us physically and, though we could not have voiced this at the time, spiritually as well. I can still see the sunlight caught in the striations of rock on the riverbank, and the osprey poised among wheeling clouds that revealed visible currents of air. I can still smell the pines and feel the crunch of fallen leaves and twigs beneath my high-top running shoes with no brand name to colonize my sensual contact with the world. Later, at the pond, I would have been embarrassed by any invocation of God or faith to explain my feelings of participation in something larger than myself, a kind of ceremony perhaps that one simply joined but did not attempt to explain. And after that, my intellect often got in the way of transcendence or vision that called assumptions about the ordinary into question. Earlier, though, in the Don Valley, I was open to speculations on all fronts about my strange sense of connection to such commonplace things as pine cones and birdsongs. God was merely another name for such questions and their origins.

The River

Before the pond and the valley there was Muskoka. I'm not speaking here of the cottages of wealth on Lake Rosseau or Lake Muskoka itself, the ones with mahogany-hulled inboard cruisers idling at their docks, and cultivated lawns stretching from screened-in porches to the water's edge. I'm not speaking of holidays of plenty wherein the natural world was at the service of those whose way of life was not altered by rhythms of wind and wave, but reinforced by emulations of city existence and the subjugation of things uncivilized.

Rather than turn west along the paved entrance into the resort town of Bracebridge, the car turns down a wood-lined gravel road to the east. Dust rises behind us to obscure our origins and discourage the search parties already forming, given our wilderness destination. I am six years old, and the name Vankoughnet with its strangely evocative sound does not have anything to do with things familiar. "He was some sort of government official," my mother tells me, but the lasting impact of the place will become larger than any image of the man. Fifteen miles from the highway, the village consists of a few houses, a tiny church, and a general store with a single-bubble gas pump out front. To my surprise, we keep going another mile or so, now beside a river whose obsidian surface hides, I am sure, all the fish of my dreams. "The Black River," mother announces, and then we are on the bridge.

It is an old trestle design with steel side girders criss-crossing to frame views of the river, and boards laid down like tracks that rattle beneath us as we pass. Downstream I catch a glimpse of a log building by the shore, brushed by pines on three sides, with a small sandy beach in front. My father stops the car, turns it off, and we get out on the middle of the bridge. At first there is nothing to replace the sound of the motor, and then I hear the rush beneath my feet, the steady hum of the rapids. Cautiously I look through the lattice-work railing, my knuckles drained of colour by my tight grip on the metal. There is only the slightest glint of white water at the tips of rocks protruding above the surface. The rest of the rapids are a dark sheen of movement that curves and falls over a smooth floor of granite without arrest. I can see this floor because the passage of water is very shallow, probably not more than a foot or two deep in most places, and the sunlight illuminates even the smallest of green fronds leaning one way in the current. "It's like a window," I say aloud, and yearn to stand on the bedrock, though I know it will be slippery, and bend and hold the river in my hands. Thirty-five years later, when I return to the same spot with my two young sons, the trestle has been replaced by a concrete span, and the log cabin has disappeared, but when I lift each of the boys to look over the edge, the window is still open and unchanged.

I spend the summer with my sister and another boy and his sister, shifting back and forth between the cabin and a weathered clapboard house at the head of a rutted lane that begins just past the bridge. The woman who looks after us is in her sixties and came to the area as a teacher during the

Depression. The one-room school in which she taught is at the foot of the lane, and in use between September and June. The house is set at the end of a field that a local farmer mows twice a year, and the borders of the field are lined with coniferous growth so thick that we are warned about taking even a few steps inside. There are black bears and snakes, we are told, and need to hear no more about forest depths, though the snakes frequent the woodpile close to the house and sun themselves in the garden behind. Nonetheless, every night before bed, we don our pyjamas and march barefoot around the field, playing sundry instruments on loan from the school music cupboard—a snare drum, cymbals, a glockenspiel, and brass cornet. Somewhere, deep in their pine domain, the bears cover their ears.

But the best of times we spend by or in the river. I learn to swim, and several weeks after my first dog-paddle efforts, I am able to step off the strand of sand and splash across the thirty yards of river, nearly all of which is over my head in depth. The rapids are too far upstream to swim to, so we climb down the bank beneath the bridge and walk out on exposed rocks to the central flow that is moving much faster than any view from above would suggest. When I put my hand in the water and cup it against the current, I cannot keep it in place. Sticks dropped on the glassy surface disappear in a flash, whirled into the main channel by a force we realize would claim us in the same way, our limbs flashing briefly before the vanishing point, though we insist if we had a canoe we could stay visible, and regale one another with stories of our paddling prowess. In the end, of course, we never shoot the rapids, but hover on the peripheries of disaster, trying to get as close as possible to the underwater drop-off, our toes gripping the bedrock while our legs withstand the build up of the river, the white surge of current often rising as high as our waists before we withdraw, checked by unaccustomed thoughts of mortality.

Upstream the water is deep and impenetrable. Two or three times a week, we walk from the house to the village to buy food, carrying the kind of quart baskets in which farmers sell their apples. The road parallels the river, but is above it, and a steep bank accompanies us on the right of our outward journey and the left of our return. The angle is such that if we slipped from the road we would tumble all the way to the water and in. The water moves slowly here, and we have an unarticulated sense of a long time passing below us. Occasionally a branch protrudes from the flat surface, on which a bird perches as if in respite from demands of wind and sky, and we wonder if this piece of flotsam has snagged on something larger and unseen or is part of a giant tree resting on the river bottom, thrusting up this one sign of its dignified but dark repose. We talk of building a raft and floating towards the rapids, but strangely it is the smooth, unreflecting section of the river at our feet, rather than the danger of white water, that deters our thoughts and plans. We make up stories of creatures in the depths, never thinking of these as projections of our childhood fears onto the natural world or of our alliance with other children down through time. Once, one of us drops a basket filled with food, and we watch it bounce downhill to disappear beneath the surface, the fruit rolling beside the container as if in a race for oblivion, the coins from our transaction at the general store scattered in gleaming array across the bank. We climb down gingerly to retrieve the survivors—bruised apples, oranges no worse for wear, and the nickels and pennies that will go in the big preserve jar on the kitchen shelf. I put my hand in the river up to the wrist, and then lift it back into the world, the water dripping from it as if from a storybook chalice. Impulsively, I cup my palm and drink from the river. The others shout down my audacity, but I am no longer afraid.

The Sea

I first saw the ocean while standing on a beach at Weymouth, England, in the spring of 1966. It has been a part of my life for so long that it is difficult to believe my childhood and youth went by without it. I had flown across the Atlantic (my first airplane ride as well) overnight, and there were clouds over the Irish Channel as we approached Heathrow from the west just after dawn. I remember my excited response to the green fields of England, the birthplace of my parents and, apart from the American shoreline at Niagara Falls, the first foreign soil I had ever glimpsed. I was coming to experience life in London and perhaps to visit family members in the north. The sea was not a factor.

It was a cold night in early May, around midnight, and the beach was deserted. I was hitchhiking through southern England, and had been rather unceremoniously dropped on the Weymouth strand by a naval officer who was anxious to get back to his nearby base. My first thoughts were to find a hostel and cup of hot tea, but then I heard the wash of water, and for some reason Canadian coasts I had never seen suddenly seemed part of my heritage. No moon or stars lit my way as I walked out on the sand, past the shuttered booths of summer commerce, guided only by the recurrent sound of breaking waves, toward something both old and new, an ancient and nascent rhythm in the heart and mind. It was so dark that when I stood on the final residue of English soil, I could see only the purling water at my feet, but I sensed whatever depths of experience and character I had acquired in my twenty years were somehow part of this visible rise and fall, and of the powerful cadence just beyond.

Since then I have lived for extended periods of time on Mediterranean islands in Spain and Greece. My blue-green submersions off those coastlines are part of a story I have told in poetry and fiction through the years, in which the ritual of language cannot be separated from the benison of salt-water memories and visions. My life in Halifax does not provide much immediate contact with the sea, despite the peninsular nature of the city, though every morning on my way to work I drive alongside the Northwest Arm and look past the fishing boats and weekend yachts to fog banks or cerulean combinations of water and sky, reminded daily of alternatives to earthbound tasks by these measures without end.

Two years ago my partner and I went looking for a vacation property in Nova Scotia and, without need for discussion, drove the coastal roads of the Northumberland Strait. We had already spent brief periods of several summers with our four—then five—young children at a friend's cottage on the far side of Pugwash. A huge tidal beach and glimpses of Prince Edward Island twenty miles away on clear days gave us a sense of space and disconnection from the turmoils of our city existence. Then the kids grew older and found the idyll less attractive, all but the youngest boy who could still get excited by tidal pools and snorkelling adventures with his parents and friends. So we bought just over an acre of oceanfront field a little closer to Halifax, with the PEI bridge in sight and a patchwork of Island fields on the northern horizon.

The first summer, we camped and walked the beach in the morning and evening light, marvelling at how it changed from week to week, the strands reshaped by the waves and tides, with new pebble formations making intricate designs on the sand. We swam in the shallows formed by a rock ledge about fifty metres offshore, the scuttling crabs magnified by our masks and the intricate fronds of underwater plants waving gently as we passed. Now we have a one-room cabin filled with cast-off but still comfortable furniture, where we wait out the rainy days. Though we can see the ocean through our windows, sometimes we move closer to sit on our cliffside bench, where we watch the movement of the water and the clouds scudding across its reflection, lost in contemplation of the immensity and of those intimations of immortality, oddly soothed by the constancy of change before us. Our son and his dog run free on the beach, and there is nowhere else we would rather be.

Coda: Viareggio

In November 2000, I attend a Canadian Studies conference in Pisa to discuss the production of a literary atlas of the Atlantic provinces. If there is a certain irony to leaving Nova Scotia to fly to Italy to begin the mapping of local writers' landscapes, there is also the anticipation of being able to see part of Tuscany. In particular, I want to visit the beach where Shelley's body had washed ashore after his drowning in July 1822. I want to pay homage because I am a writer and teacher of literature and because his life and work have touched me deeply. A colleague drives me to the tourist trap of Viareggio, but in this off-season the hotels are virtually empty and the beach deserted. She remains in the car while I walk out on the strand and leave the buildings behind me, facing a sea whose turbulence is without precedence in my experience. Cross-currents and rip tides are driven by a ferocious wind into the base of mountainous waves that twist and turn on one another in crashing disarray. Though particles of grit sting my face and my eyelashes are soon caked with salt, still I look for Shelley, his tiny pleasure craft long since crushed, his body tumbling toward me like a bottled message from the past. But the sea delivers something else. I am hunkered down, my body slightly turned against the wind, my eyes fixed on an eruptive patterning of waves that have formed around a submerged formation of rock, when the proverbial "rogue" catches me unawares. Suddenly the water is *behind* me, filling a declivity I had not noticed, and I am cut off from dry land on a rapidly dissolving island of sand. My first instinct is to plunge in over my head and make for shore, but then I realize the encircling current is moving out to sea and, encumbered by my winter clothes, I will die in the attempt. There is no point in shouting into the roar of wind and wave, so I stay crouched down and, strangely, peacefully, think again of Shelley. He does not appear, but I have a small sense of his small sense of self before the storm, and that above all this *is* a place to die. The water behind me recedes. My colleague hits her car horn, but for a long time I do not move. I am at home.

7

Who Cares about the Meadow?
The Changing Conversation around Religion and Ecology

Anne Marie Dalton

Sometime in the mid-1970s, I picked up some papers lying around Holy Cross Centre (later to be called Holy Cross Centre for Ecology and Spirituality) in Port Burwell, Ontario. The papers were written by Thomas Berry, by now well known as one of the pioneer voices on the relationship of religion to the ecological crisis. As a child of the 1960s and a student of biology, I was well aware of the ecological crisis but until that point had not thought of it as a religious problem. Thomas Berry made sense: the ecological crisis, could not be solved by technocrats or even by scientists alone. It was primarily a deep cultural, hence religious, crisis. In fact, Berry made enough sense to me that the rest of my academic life took shape from that moment. I would go on to study with Thomas Berry, later write a dissertation and a book on his thought, and continue to follow the development of thought on the relationship of religion to ecology, much of it inspired by his visionary essays and talks. This essay takes its starting point from Berry's essay, "The Meadow across the Creek," in his book *The Great Work*.

In his essay, Berry reminisces about the impact of a memorable moment that would define for him the "feeling for what is real and worthwhile in life" (1999, 13). This moment was his first encounter with a meadow across the creek from his new family home on the outskirts of Greensboro, North Carolina. It was late spring in North Carolina and the meadow was covered with white lilies emerging from tall grass. Crickets and birds could be heard.

73

The sky above was blue with drifting white clouds and, for the eleven-year-old Berry, the whole ambiance was magical. Berry moves from this description to a quite sombre reflection on the disappearance of that particular meadow, along with many others, and the human responsibility for the future that this reality presents. He links them with a statement about the crucial significance of this childhood moment and the sensitivities it represents in his life's work.

> This early experience, it seems, has become normative for me throughout the entire range of my thinking. Whatever preserves and enhances this meadow in the natural cycles of its transformation is good; whatever opposes the meadow or negates it is not good. My life orientation is that simple. It is also that pervasive. It applies in economics and political orientation as well as in education and religion. (1999, 13)

And indeed it is true. Berry's essays through the almost forty years of his writing on the ecological crisis can be seen as explications of the orientation and pervasiveness that he sums up right here. What do science, religion, economics, education, law, political structures, communities, and individuals have to do to permit the existence and self-fulfillment of "the meadow," understood in its concrete physical reality as well as in its metaphorical extension to the whole natural world?[1]

While Berry's vision and challenge continue to remain relevant, the conversation between religion and ecology has been a dynamic and changing one. Not only have partners to the conversation changed, but the nature of what one means by "meadow" and how one speaks about and cares for the meadow theologically and religiously continues to change. Hence, the conversation between religion and ecology (or more properly among the religions and ecology) has become more and more complex. My intent here is to sketch some of the contours of the changing conversation in hope of finding a path that is going to increase ecological awareness and responsibility from the viewpoint of religious praxis. For various reasons, the conversation that arose with the latest wave of awareness of the ecological crisis (starting in the 1960s) began, by and large, within Christianity first, so this essay will follow the development primarily from the Christian perspective, but not exclusively.[2]

Berry's argument was that the ecological crisis was primarily religiously based in the Christian tradition. This was so because biblical notions in the West encouraged a radical disjunction between human life and the rest of the natural world. Beliefs about the sublime vocation of humankind, the transcendence of God above the natural world, and the promise of a happier and truer life in the supernatural realm all led to a disregard for the natural world. On a more positive note, however, Berry also maintained that all the great religions had contributed in the past to a more benign attitude toward the natural world than existed in modern times, and were still capable of contributing to a comprehensive cosmology or story of existence which made for a more congenial relationship between humans and their cosmos. Furthermore, he believed that in contemporary times such a story could be intentionally constructed from an integration of the scientific account of the evolution of the universe and the spiritual insights of traditional religions.[3] This conviction led to the 1992 publication of *The Universe Story*, co-authored with mathematical physicist Brian Swimme. Berry also consistently challenged the traditional religions to take seriously their responsibilities to articulate a religious ethic to confront the ecological crisis within their own traditions. The new universe story, he proposed, was the context within which religions could articulate their unique responses to the crisis.

It is arguably Berry's first contention of regarding Christianity's complicity in the ecological crisis, together with a much less nuanced and more hard-hitting approach represented by Lynn White, that gave the most energy to the Christian reflection on the ecological crisis. Biblical scholars within the Christian tradition began delving with rigour into the sacred text in search of ecological teaching. Works such as Bernhard W. Anderson's *From Creation to New Creation: Old Testament Perspectives* and, in a more popular vein, Richard Cartwright Austin's series, *Environmental Theology*, gave a balance to early reductive accounts, such as White's, of biblical teaching on ecology. H. Paul Santmire wrote a compelling analysis of the ambiguity of the Christian tradition with regard to ecological teaching, *The Travail of Nature: The Ambiguous Ecological Promise of Christian Thought*. Defenses and extensions of creation theology multiplied. Representatives of virtually all branches of Christian theology and within virtually all Christian denominations added their analyses to the growing volume of ecological writing. The focus in all cases was on the Bible and written traditions of Christian history. In these cases, the meadow could be understood to be the earth (mostly, or sometimes the entire cosmos), and what constituted the earth was assumed to be clearly understood and the same for all. While most theologians did attempt to respond to the concern for social justice, voices from the developing world or any compelling critique based on race, class, and gender were to come later.[4]

While Christian theologians were at work mining that tradition, voices were raised from within other religious traditions. Berry himself had indicated that each tradition contained wisdom regarding human relationships to the natural world.[5] Some, like the aboriginal traditions, stood out as believing in and practising a much more intimate presence with the earth than the mainline traditions. Hence, there arose articles and books on Islam and the Environment, Buddhism and ecology, Hinduism, and Judaism, as well as on the aboriginal traditions.[6] This kind of work is very likely to continue within the traditions, but perhaps reached a climax in the Harvard project, *Ecology and the World Religions*, and its large publications.[7] This project covered both large general themes and more particular ones within the traditions, recovering and reconstructing traditional teachings and practices in light of the new awareness of the plight of the natural world. In *Buddhism and Ecology*, for instance, topics range from a general consideration of a Buddhist philosophy of nature to the role of a Buddhist monastery in Thailand in promoting a green society there.[8]

As religionists and theologians were doing their work, so were scientists, many of whom were not content with science as usual. Cosmologists and astronomers were making new discoveries and some of them were awestruck by the immensity of the universe as it now appeared to them. Space exploration was producing images of the "blue planet," the small fragile orb floating in a sea of darkness. This work, combined with warnings about the degraded state of the earth from colleagues in environmental, atmospheric, and life sciences, provoked an activism among scientists. Some of this activism called for collaboration with religionists, theologians, and ethicists. In 1992, leaders and scholars of religion and science met at a Washington, DC, "Religion and Science for the Environment" conference, and released a statement committing them to work together for the preservation of the earth.[9] I was at that event and experienced what was perhaps the high point of optimism for those of us concerned about the ecological crisis. Despite a few discordant voices from the clergy, indicating that there might be a racial and class dimension to how the ecological crisis was affecting people, the general tone was of universal concern for the state of the earth and the prospects of a viable future for all our children.

In 1995, similar symposia were initiated by the religion, science, and environment group for the preservation of the Black Sea. Reporting on the second of these symposia, Jenny Banks Bryer, one of the participating scientists, noted, "the scientists and politicians present felt very strongly that the environment could not be meaningfully discussed without the full consideration of the moral, ethical and spiritual values implicit in responsible ecological and environmental policy" (1999, 70). Such events, as well as the increasing interest in the whole question of science and value by scientific organizations such as the American Association for the Advancement of Science, gave significant recognition to the role of religions in confronting the ecological crisis.

Besides these more high-powered efforts, interdisciplinary conversations multiplied between religionists and scientists, as well as artists, philosophers, and others. In Canada, colloquia took place from 1980 to 2000, which brought Thomas Berry into conversation with representatives from different academic disciplines, various religious believers, scholars, and activist groups at the Centre for Ecology and Spirituality in Port Burwell, Ontario. Economists, educators, Native spiritual leaders, artists, organic farmers, and feminists considered the relevance of Thomas Berry's work across society.

In my own development in this field, all of these occasions have played their parts. I joined in many of the conversations that tried to bring together the insights of the sciences and the religions to better confront the ecological crisis. From the beginning, this was an interdisciplinary and difficult path. Science and religion were not easy partners historically! In terms of the ecological crisis, however, it was not this collaboration that raised the most pressing questions about the direction of the ecological and environmental movements. These came from the "underdeveloped" countries (the economic South) and were given a particular emphasis by the women represented in that group.

From the beginning of Christian theologians' attempts to deal with the ecological crisis, there has been persistent concern on the part of theologians involved in social justice issues. In dialogue with Thomas Berry at the Centre for Ecology and Spirituality in 1986, for instance, Canadian theologian Gregory Baum commented that the radical ecological program must be socially and politically active as well.[10] Attempts were made to bring together the two concerns, social justice and ecological responsibility. One of the earliest theologians to take up this agenda explicitly was Rosemary Radford Ruether. Ruether combined the insights of liberation theology, ecological concern, and feminism. She wrote: "Any ecological ethic must always take into account the structures of social domination and exploitation that mediate domination of nature and prevent concern for the welfare of the whole community" (1983, 91). In the postscript to the same work, she illuminated the concrete relationship that exists between injustice towards the poor and the rape of the earth: "The labor of dominated bodies, dominated peoples—women, peasants, workers—mediate for those who rule the fruits of the earth. The toil of laboring bodies provides the tools through which the earth is despoiled and left desolate. Through the raped bodies the earth is raped. Those who enjoy the goods distance themselves from the destruction" (1983, 263).

To those like Ruether, for whom concern for the ecological crisis had started to engage structural problems of social justice, perhaps the watershed event was the 1992 United Nations Conference on Environment and Development (the Earth Summit) held in Rio de Janeiro, Brazil. For many ecologists and environmentalists, this summit was a sign of hope; never had so many world leaders assembled for the sole purpose of responding to the worldwide environmental crisis.[11] For others, however, especially for many of those from the economic South, the summit represented the co-option by the world economic hegemony of the environmental movements that for the most part had gathered impetus in the counter-cultural movements of the 1960s and 1970s. Environmental problems, they accused, were formulated in terms of Northern interests and, likewise, the proposed solutions primarily and even exclusively benefited the North. It was for them what Tom Athanasiou called "a defining moment in the evolution of green-washing" (1996, 10). Green was not what it seemed. On the one hand, the rhetoric of the environment had succeeded in creating a public conversational space for serious ecological concern; on the other hand, that space now seemed to many to be vacuous.[12]

Among the voices that gained strength from the Earth Summit experience were those of women of the South. Women's involvement in the ecological movements had been strong since the beginning. Ecofeminists claimed that the same societal and cultural forces that had oppressed women in the past had also oppressed nature. Some claimed a special innate closeness between women and nature. These women often placed themselves outside mainline religious structures and looked to nature or to the recovery of goddess religions for their spirituality.[13] The women of the South, however, like the South in general, were late to the scene. As women of colour had in the North, the women of the South entered the conversation with a certain annoyance and even anger at the presupposition of Northern women that we spoke for them. Within the feminist movement itself, voices like those of bell hooks, in *Ain't I a Woman: Black Women and Feminism,* had already differentiated themselves from white, middle-class feminists. In 1988, the Indian physicist and philosopher, Vandana Shiva, published *Staying Alive,* in which she illuminated for Western readers the special environmental concerns of poor women in the developing world and their plight at the hands of "development." On the basis of her Hindu belief in Prakriti, the feminine principle of nature, she argued for a unique status for women in relation to the natural world. Others would deny such an essentialist stand and locate women's closeness to nature within the social construction of gender roles that brought more women than men into close contact with the natural world. To return to the earlier metaphor, women not only cared for the meadow as much as men, in fact they cared for it more. In addition, while the destruction of that meadow threatens all human life, the threat is greater for women, especially for poor women, than it is for men. Hence, women challenged the religion and ecology conversation both from the spiritual contexts on the fringes of mainline religions and from the material contexts of their poverty and struggle for subsistence.

The interventions of the South in the periods before, during, and after the Summit were not a big surprise to environmentalists and ecologists, or to the religion-ecology conversation. The magnitude of the event and the intensity of these interventions, however, catapulted the concerns of the South onto centre stage. The credibility of the North's concern for the environment was at stake. The big questions included: How can you denounce population growth in the South and continue the skyrocketing increase in consumerism in the North? Having reaped the benefits of flagrant use of natural resources both in the North and in the colonized South, how could the North have any kind of authentic voice in calling for the protection of rain forests, coral reefs, and wildlife habitats in the South? Furthermore, the rapid globalization efforts and structural adjustment programs of international development organizations were controlled by the rich corporations of the North and were wreaking havoc with both environmental and social programs in the South. The explication of the implications of these questions and concerns is beyond the scope of this essay, but there are many works dealing with these subjects.[14] The point is that events such as the Earth Summit, and the overall failure of most development efforts to improve the quality of life for most of the earth's poor, led to a concerted re-evaluation of the assumptions underlying the involvement of rich nations in the lives of the poor.

In a more positive light, for those willing to look and listen with empathetic eyes and ears, the diversity of the earth's communities became more apparent and compelling when more voices were raised. The naiveté that once painted all aboriginal communities with the brush of environmental "holiness," and saw wilderness preservation of the North as the panacea for ecosystem sustainability around the world, was recognized for what it is. As anthropologist Kay Milton concludes of the romanticization of the indigenous peoples' environmental ethic by the dominant culture: "It is unrealistic to lump together all indigenous and traditional peoples and claim that they understand their environments in ways that contrast sharply with Western models. Indigenous and traditional societies embrace a wide variety of ecological practices, which generate a diversity of environmental perspectives, some of which are as ambiguous and contradictory as Western concepts of 'nature'" (87–88).

Besides the material context of globalization, the ecological movements are now confronted with the pervasive implications of philosophical discussions around the notion of social construction in all its variegated postmodern forms. Not only the notions of gender roles, sexuality, and development, but also the very concepts of nature and body themselves are considered products of social production. There are varying degrees of skepticism around whether or not there is some reality to "nature" or "meadow" that transcends or grounds our human perceptions of what these are.[15] On the positive side, this discussion has led to increased sensitivity to different religious and cultural voices on the subject of environmental responsibility. On the negative side, it has been argued that postmodernism has introduced a new kind of imperialism that denies subjectivity to peoples and cultures as well as reality to nature.[16] For the most part, religious scholars continue to address the relevance of their particular religions to ecology by grounding their arguments in sacred texts. However, there are also the emerging religious voices of those who see the value of considering what nature, and hence the ecological crisis, means in each particular place with its own peculiar forms of human-earth interactions.[17]

Science, in substantial ways, was the foundation of the environmental movement, in terms of our reliance on scientific accounts of the state of the earth and expertise in testing, predicting, and recommending technical solutions. Recently, however, science itself has been subject to the critique of social constructionists. The net effect of this development is ambiguous. On the one hand, such a relativization of scientific expertise places science among other human activities and allows space for the recognition of other kinds of knowledge (such as that of traditional and local cultures) as relevant to the solution of ecological problems. On the other hand, the ecological and environmental movements have lost the "arguability of science," the non-contestable data to support their stands on everything from climate change to population control.[18] So, for instance, discussions around climate change and what best to do about it can be diverted around such questions as whether pollution has much at all to do with increasing temperatures or if the planet is in fact warming up.

All religions teach about "the creation." The mythic presentations of the events around the creation of the cosmos generally carry values and principles for living on earth within set limits and with definable responsibilities. These values and principles are the basis on which religion enters the conversation with ecology. Religions remain relevant in the world insofar as they address the promises and problems of life. This is also true of ecology and religion discussions. The development of religious teachings to meet the ecological crisis remains dynamic and relevant by the continuous confrontation between, and integration or rejection of, insights and activities in the broader culture. The growing complexity of the factors related to the ecological crisis outlined in this essay is the stuff of religious reflection on the ecological crisis. Each religion may well adapt to these factors differently, but they all will have to contend with environmental degradation, resource depletion, species extinction, global warming, and the web of social arrangements within which these issues are embedded.

Religious ecologists have attempted to influence the cultural perceptions grounding the human destruction and disregard for the physical world. Cultural perceptions are powerful tools both for the entrenchment of traditional views as well as for change. Hence, we have the reinvention of rituals, the recovery of ancient symbols and practices that celebrated the earth and cosmic cycles, such as solstices and lunar phases, and the establishment of counter-cultural communities which emphasize simplicity of lifestyle and more friendly earth-human relationships. The nature of the religious conversation has changed most in the realization of the ways in which societal and global structures skillfully and efficiently co-opt even the very rhetoric, symbols, and activities that were intended to undermine the destructive potential of those structures.[19] Hence the need for continuous critical reflection to inform and enrich religious thought and practice.

The conversation between religion and ecology has changed immensely since the young Thomas Berry encountered the beauty of the meadow, and since I first encountered his vision. In the past four years, I have been involved in a project to establish environmental programs at three universities in China and Vietnam. While driving from the airport into Hanoi for the first time, I looked with studious interest at the surroundings. There were large rice patties scattered with Vietnamese men, women, and children in their traditional straw hats working the fields. Were these the meadows of

Vietnam? The neighbouring properties were modern factories. The fields were criss-crossed with modern highways. Like Berry's meadow in North Carolina, these too were encroached upon and may be disappearing. Equipped with my academic tools—the critical analyses, the rhetoric, and the postmodern doubts—I saw among the Vietnamese workers the global reach of corporate world power and wondered about my inability to know this different reality. From a religious-ecological perspective, the enlargement and intensification of the conversation about the natural world and its human inhabitants can have an immobilizing effect. Is there nothing one can say outside the extremely circumscribed locale of one's own existence? But the urgency is to opt for the more life-giving rejection of this stance of extreme relativism and pluralism.[20] Some action in the 1920s to save a small meadow in North Carolina could well have repercussions in the rice paddies of Vietnam.

For me, some of the most promising engagement of religion in the contemporary ecological crisis has paid attention to the concrete and local as part of the larger vision of an earth to be healed and handed on to the future. One such example is the recent work of The Centre for Religion and Society at the University of Victoria. The publication *Just Fish* resulted from research in local communities by religionists, sociologists, and others examining the effects of the collapse of the fishing industry in eastern Canada.[21] Their efforts represent an instance of seeing the ecological and social crises as one, and doing so in a way that recognizes the variety of concrete interactions between human communities and the ecosystems of which they are a part. They attend to the fact that human interaction goes beyond the men and women present to the setting they inhabit. The forces that killed the fishery were by and large beyond the control of those for whom it was a traditional livelihood. Such is the case in virtually all communities today. This, more than any other realization, is likely to mark the religious reflection on the ecological crisis in the near future.

What is moving forward in the ecology and religion conversation? In terms of efforts likely to be effective in the influence of policy and change, the growing attention to the concrete and particular instances of the global ecological crisis is both exciting and hopeful. It is there, perhaps, that the compassionate and ethical side of religious reflection can be of best use. So the meadow is the place to start; and, as it was in Berry's case, perhaps it is the particular and the concrete that inspire both the vision and the caring.

Notes

1 Many of Berry's essays are published in his two books, *The Great Work* (New York: Random House, 1999) and *Dream of the Earth* (San Francisco: Sierra Club, 1988). For a comprehensive listing of his works up to 1998, see the bibliography in my book, *A Theology for the Earth: The Contributions of Thomas Berry and Bernard Lonergan* (Ottawa: University of Ottawa Press, 1999).

2 As indicated below, the early relevant literature reveals a sense of responsibility by Christians for the ecological crisis, as Christianity has and still does inform movements of imperialism and globalization throughout the world. Controversy over the degree of culpability of Christianity is part of the discussion.

3 Cf. Berry, "The New Story," in *Dream of the Earth*, 123-37.

4 Charlene Spretnak, *The Spiritual Dimensions of Green Politics* (Santa Fe: Bear, 1986); Richard Cartwright Austin, *Hope for the Land* (Abingdon, VA: Creekside Press, 1988-91); Philip N. Joranson, *Cry of the Environment: Rebuilding the Christian Creation Tradition* (Santa Fe: Bear, 1984); Charles M. Murphy, *At Home on Earth: Foundations of a Catholic Ethic of the Environment* (New York: Crossroads, 1989); Ian C. Bradley, *God Is Green: Ecology for Christians* (New York: Doubleday, 1992); Douglas J. Hall, *Imaging God: Dominion as Stewardship* (Grand Rapids, MI: W.B. Eerdmans, 1986); John B. Cobb, *Is It Too Late? A Theology of Ecology* (Beverley Hills, CA: Bruce, 1972); Gibson Winter, *Liberating Creation* (New York: Crossroad, 1981); James Gustafson, *Ethics from a Theocentric Perspective* (Chicago: University of Chicago Press, 1981); Ian C. Barbour, "An Ecological Ethic," *The Christian Century*, October 7, 1970, 1180-84; Donald E. Cowan, "Genesis and Ecology: Does Subdue Mean Plunder?" op. cit. 1188-90; James J. McGiven, "Ecology and the Bible," *The Ecumenist* 8, 5 (July–August 1970): 69-71; André Beauchamp, "Reflexions théologiques à propos d'une éthique de l'environment," *Science et Esprit* 32, 2 (1980): 217-33.

5 Cf. Thomas Berry, "The Cosmology of Religion," in *Pluralism and Oppression: The Annual Publication of the College Theology Society* 34 (1988): 100-13.

6 Cf. Eugene C. Hargrove, ed., *Religion and the Environmental Crisis* (Athens, GA: University of Georgia Press, 1986). This volume contains essays by representatives of most of the major religious traditions.

7 This project was conducted from 1996-98 at the Harvard University Center for the Study of World Religions. Publication of the papers presented is continuing with the following volumes already in print: *Christianity and Ecology: Seeking the Well-Being of Earth and Human*, Dieter T. Hessel and Rosemary Radford Ruether, eds. (Cambridge, MA: Harvard University Center for the Study of World Religions Publications, 2000); *Buddhism and Ecology: The Interconnection of Dharma and Deeds*, Mary Evelyn Tucker and Duncan Ryūken Williams, eds. (Cambridge, MA: Harvard University Center for the Study of World Religion, 1997); and *Confucianism and Ecology: The Interrelation of Heaven, Earth, and Humans*, Mary Evelyn Tucker and John Berthong, eds. (Cambridge, MA: Harvard University Center for the Study of World Religion, 1998).

8 Malcolm David Eckel, "Is There a Buddhist Philosophy of Nature?" and Leslie E. Sponsel and Poranee Natadecha-Sponsel, "A Theoretical Analysis of the Poten-

tial Contribution of the Monastic Community in Promoting a Green Society in Thailand" in *Buddhism and Ecology*.

9 For a summary of this event as well as for the statement itself, see Anne Marie Dalton, "Religion and Science," *Living Light* (Fall 1992): 14–26.

10 Gregory Baum, "The Grand Vision: It Needs Social Action," in *Thomas Berry and the New Cosmology*, Anne Lonergan and Caroline Richards, eds. (Mystic, CT: Twenty-Third Publications, 1987), 51–56. This book contains the responses of a number of theologians to Berry's thought during a dialogue held in 1983.

11 Cf. Steve Lerner, *Beyond the Earth Summit: Conversations with Advocates of Sustainable Development* (Bolinas, CA: Commonweal, 1992).

12 Cf. articles in *Global Ecology: A New Arena of Political Conflict*, Wolfgang Sachs, ed. (Halifax, NS: Fernwood, 1993). See also, Simon Upton, "Roadblocks to Agenda 21: A Government Perspective," *Earth Summit 2002: A New Deal*, Felix Dodds, ed. (United Nations Environment and Development–UK Committee, 2000, rev. ed. 2001), 3–20, as well as other essays in this volume that show the ambiguous fallout from the Rio conference as far as the developing countries are concerned.

13 For a sample of ecofeminist thought, cf. *Reweaving the World: The Emergence of Ecofeminism*, Irene Diamond and Gloria Feman Orenstein, eds. (San Francisco: Sierra Club Books, 1990).

14 Cf. *Global Ecology*; and Rosi Braidotti, *Women, the Environment and Sustainable Development: Toward a Theoretical Synthesis* (London: Zed Books, 1994).

15 For a good overview of the problems this kind of postmodernist view presents, see Charlene Spretnak, *States of Grace* (San Francisco: Harper, 1991). For a more recent discussion, see a dissertation by Nancie Erhart, *Moral Habitat: Ethos and Agency for the Sake of the Earth* (Ann Arbor, MI: UNI dissertation services, 2002), 9–10, 75–85.

16 Cf. Ziauddin Sardar, *Postmodernism and the Other: The New Imperialism of Western Culture* (London: Pluto Press, 1998).

17 Cf. Chung Hyun Kyung, *Struggle to Be Sun Again: Introducing Asian Women's Theology* (Maryknoll, NY: Orbis Books, 1997); see also, essays in *Earth Habitat: Eco-Injustice and the Church's Response*, Dieter Hessel and Larry Rasmussen, eds. (Minneapolis: Fortress Press, 2001).

18 The term "arguability of science" occurs in George Myerson and Yvonne Rydin, *The Language of the Environment: A New Rhetoric* (London: University College Press, 1996), 213.

19 Cf. articles integrating social justice and ecology, feminism and ecology, globalization and environmentalism, etc., in the Religions of the World and Ecology series. Samples include Daniel C. Maguire, "Population, Consumption, Ecology: The Triple Problematic," Rosemary Radford Ruether, "Ecofeminism: The Challenge to Theology," and Marthinus L. Danecel, "Earthkeeping Churches at the African Grassroots" in *Christianity and Ecology*; Huey-hi Li, "Some Thoughts on Confucianism and Ecofeminism" in *Confucianism and Ecology*; and Kenneth Kraft, "Nuclear Ecology and Engaged Buddhism" in *Buddhism and Ecology*. See also, Heather Eaton, "Ecological Feminist Theology" in *Theology for Earth Community: A Field Guide*, Dieter T. Hessel, ed. (Maryknoll, NY: Orbis Books, 1996).

20 For a response to this postmodern query from a religious and ecological perspective, see references in note 15.
21 *Just Fish: Ethics and Canadian Marine Fisheries*, Harold Coward, Rosemary Ommer, and Tony Pitcher, eds. (St. John's, NL: ISER Books, 2000). See also, Peggy M. Shepard, "Issues of Community Empowerment," *Earth Habitat: Eco-Injustice and the Church's Response* (Minneapolis: Fortress Press, 2001), 159–71.

Works Cited

Anderson, Bernhard W. *From Creation to New Creation: Old Testament Perspectives*. Minneapolis: Fortress, 1994.

Athanasiou, Tom. *Divided Planet: The Ecology of Rich and Poor*. Boston: Little, Brown, 1996.

Austin, Richard Cartwright. *Hope for the Land: Nature in the Bible*. Atlanta: John Knox Press, 1988.

Barney, Gerald O. *Global 2000 Revisited: What Should We Do?* A report on the critical issues of the twenty-first century prepared for the 1993 Parliament of World's Religions. Arlington, VA: Public Interest Publications, 1993.

Baum, Gregory. "The Grand Vision: It Needs Social Action." In *Thomas Berry and the New Cosmology*, ed. Anne Lonergan and Caroline Richard. Mystic, CT: Twenty-Third Publications. 1987. 51–56.

Berry, Thomas. *The Great Work: Our Way into the Future*. New York: Random House, 1999.

———. *Dream of the Earth*. San Francisco: Sierra Club, 1988.

Bryer, Jenny Banks. "Documentation: Religion, Science and the Environment." Symposium II: The Black Sea in Crisis, 20-28 September 1997. *Islam and Christian-Muslim Relations* 10, 1 (1999): 69–76.

Chung Hyun Kyung. *Struggle to Be Sun Again: Introducing Asian Women's Theology*. Maryknoll, NY: Orbis, 1997.

Cooper, David Edward and Joy A. Palmer, eds. *Spirit of the Environment*. New York: Routledge, 1998.

Dalton, Anne Marie. *A Theology for the Earth: The Contributions of Thomas Berry and Bernard Lonergan*. Ottawa: University of Ottawa Press, 1999.

Eaton, Heather. "Ecological Feminist Theology." In *Theology for Earth Community: A Field Guide*, ed. Dieter T. Hessel. Maryknoll, NY: Orbis, 1996.

Eckel, Malcolm David. "Is There a Buddhist Philosophy of Nature?" In *Buddhism and Ecology: The Interconnection of Dharma and Deeds*, ed. Mary Evelyn Tucker, and Duncan Ryüken Williams. Cambridge, MA: Harvard University Center for the Study of World Religions, 1997.

Hessel, Dieter T., and Rosemary Radford Ruether, eds. *Christianity and Ecology: Seeking the Well-Being of Earth and Human*. Cambridge. MA: Harvard University Center for the Study of World Religions, 2000.

Hessel, Dieter, and Larry Rasmussen, eds. *Earth Habitat: Eco-Injustice and the Church's Response*. Minneapolis: Fortress, 2001.

hooks, bell. *Ain't I a Woman? Black Women and Feminism*. Boston, MA: South End Press, 1981.

Merchant, Carolyn. *The Death of Nature: Women, the Environment, and the Scientific Revolution*. New York: Harper & Row, 1980.

Milton, Kay. "Nature and the Environment in Indigenous and Traditional Cultures." In *Spirit of the Environment*, ed. David Edward Cooper and Joy A. Palmer. New York: Routledge, 1998. 87–99.

Ruether, Rosemary Radford. *Sexism and God-talk: Toward a Feminist Theology*. Boston: Beacon, 1983.

Sardar, Ziauddin. *Postmodernism and the Other: The New Imperialism of Western Culture*. London: Pluto, 1998.

Santmire, H. Paul. *The Travail of Nature: The Ambiguous Ecological Promise of Christian Thought*. Philadelphia: Fortress, 1985.

Shiva, Vandana. *Staying Alive: Ecology and Development*. London: Zed Books and New Delhi: Kali for Women, 1988.

Sponsel, Leslie E., and Poranee Natadecha-Sponsel. "A Theoretical Analysis of the Potential Contribution of the Monastic Community in Promoting a Green Society in Thailand." In *Buddhism and Ecology: The Interconnection of Dharma and Deeds*, ed. Tucker and Williams.

Swimme, Brian, and Thomas Berry. *The Universe Story*. San Francisco: Harper-Collins, 1992.

White, Lynn Jr., "Historical Roots of Our Ecologic [sic] Crisis." *Science* 155 (1967): 1203–207.

8

Toward an Ecofeminist Phenomenology of Nature
Trish Glazebrook

I grew up in Alberta, and spent many happy days backpacking in the Rockies. On longer trips, I kept a journal. Here are a couple of excerpts that capture some of the things that struck me most deeply about the natural world:

July 29
Fell in river crossing. Hauled out with minor dignity damage. Guess the rope was a good idea after all. Sun came out just in time to take the edge off icy chill of glacial run-off. Thanks, Apollo, owe you one!

Stalked by grizz. Twice left steaming pile of feces ahead of us so we'd know he knows. If you ate two of me, it wouldn't make that much shit. Thanks for the warning, big guy. Guess he's not hungry. Don't worry—we have no desire to stick around. Lucky we haven't transgressed the inner sanctum! Passed marked tree. Assumed edge of territory as no more signs.

July 30
Day off to relax, treat blisters, and check out local sights. Had breakfast (cut-throat trout, mmmmm....) watching avalanches come down between the shoulders of the five sisters. They send off tiny clouds from their crags, and even from the next mountain, I catch the snowy scent. A flutterby gets caught in my tea, and when it's rescued, it clambers up on a leaf to dry in the sun. I've seen that before, but the dimensions are different.

The biggest sister rumbles discontent and another massive hunk of snow and ice comes crashing down. I feel my mountain shake. What she fails to notice could wipe most buildings into oblivion. Between avalanches, all is still.

Or is it? Beneath the imperturbable silence is a constant hum, like a shadow flitting across the edge of my vision. It's the last river, and the next one; it's a random breeze through pine needles; it's a thousand tiny insects (and some disturbingly large horseflies!) buzzing about their business, as if each is the centre of its own universe and has no time for wandering hikers—unless we look tasty. In the end, I fear we won't be devoured dramatically by some large carnivore, but consumed mundanely by a billion insects.

These passages draw attention to insights that have remained with me and now inform what I have come to describe as an ecofeminist phenomenology of nature.

First, the apparent stillness of nature conceals a seething buzz of movement—the natural world is a ceaseless symphony of interdependent processes. Second, I experience myself not as conqueror of the natural world, but as part of it. I eat the trout I catch, but also I could be a grizzly's lunch, and am often in fact a meal for many insects. My place in the system is member, not master. Third, on the one hand, nature provides everything I need to live, as if I am cared for. There are things for me to eat and there is shelter (though I carry a tent, and once we choppered in chainsaws and built a cabin). The sun even comes out on occasion just when I need it. One day, I suspected humour when the same convection cloud repeatedly rose up the mountain I was climbing, cooled, and descended again to rain on me several times.

Yet, on the other hand, nature is indifferent to my needs, especially with respect to the weather. I have walked through days of rain and woken in tents collapsed by snow. It is for me to be careful not to hang around where a rockslide or avalanche is about to come down. Once, a fellow-hiker fell into a melt-hole on a glacier while trying to read a map in a blizzard. Luckily his pack and elbows caught the edge. One of us got the tent up and lit the Coleman stove in the few moments it took the rest of us to haul him out and peel off his pants, already freezing stiff. We gave him hot tea, he slept for sixteen hours, and we went on the next morning under a glorious blue sky. Nature gives me all I need to survive, even thrive, but is at the same time an indifferent death trap.

The key to survival is to pay close attention. Nature moves incessantly and is in constant conversation with me. I listen carefully. I look attentively at the signs and respect natural process. A dwarf, scrambling around the ankles of a giant, I cannot bend nature to my will. But as long as I am open to what is going on around me, I can work with nature to get safely to where I am going. Nature does not co-operate with me, but I can reach my goal if I co-operate with nature.

Back in the (not always civil) city, I began to realize that cultural paradigms of nature do no justice to my growing sense of respect for nature's incessant and purposeful activity. Rather, hegemonic Western ideologies of domination, control, and manipulation displace alternatives sustained over centuries. So-called Green Revolution development projects replace traditional agriculture. Fields are not left fallow, but flooded with fertilizers. Multiple-use farming and forestry practices that encourage biodiversity and minimize insect and weed damage are replaced by monocultures requiring herbicides and insecticides that in fact promote stronger strains of insects and weeds. Western culture does not respect natural process, but instead seeks confrontationally to harness and master nature. In response, I have taken what I learned in the Canadian wilderness and developed what I call "erotics" of nature.

These are erotics because they begin with love. In my case, they stem from my individual, existential love of nature. I suspect this may be the case for all erotics of nature: they arise from individual experience. But I pluralize erotics as this need not be the case, and even if it were, people's experiences of nature are many and different. I actively choose inclusivity and pluralism. Diversity permeates the human experience and is as healthy for thinking as it is for ecosystems. Furthermore, I would like erotics of nature to grow beyond individuals' love for wilderness into policy and social practice. That is, I would like to love nature not just as a single self, but to manifest my love culturally in social institutions, as marriage culturally manifests erotic love between partners.

Pornography and prostitution are, of course, also cultural institutions of the erotic. They indicate an underlying ideology of domination that fails to respect the whole, autonomous person, but rather turns the beloved into an object at the mercy of the desires of the other. Likewise, science and technology make natural entities into objects to be controlled and manipulated for human ends. I envision an alternative ideology of nature—erotics that play into policy and practice by respecting natural process and co-operating with nature rather than attempting to subjugate it. The philosophy I continue to develop for these erotics is an ecofeminist phenomenology of nature.

In writing toward this ecofeminist phenomenology, I first argue that phage therapy, recently revived in Western medical research, works with rather than against nature. I then provide an analysis of the intellectual history of the West to trace the logic of domination at work in science, which I argue relies on metaphysical and epistemological principles of universality that favour a priori theorizing over attentive observation of natural process. I suggest alternative practices on the basis of Aristotle's and Goethe's scientific methodologies, and draw attention in particular to their insight that nature is teleological, in order to suggest that sustainable technology is based on science that respects natural teleology. That is, ecologically sound science and technology work in accord with nature's ends rather than attempting to conquer it. I then explain how this view is both eco-feminist and phenomenological by sketching an answer to the question, what is nature? I end with a personal anecdote, and then I put the computer away and go for a walk. I am horrified at how much working on environmental philosophy forces me indoors to a highly technologized space!

Bacteriophages

In a discomforting scene from Michael Ondaatje's novel *The English Patient*, the protagonist's burns are treated with bacteriophagic (bacteria-eating) worms rather than pharmaceutically. Antibiotics exploit their host and cause a growing variety of human health complications. Most importantly, they promote stronger strains of bacteria that resist treatment. Bacteria are natural phenomena and thus capable of adapting to human intervention, so that they remain one step ahead of technological manipulation. Bacteriophages, an alternative to antibiotic therapy, are "good" bacteria that eat "bad" bacteria by hijacking their cellular machinery. They are an example of medical technology that works with rather than against nature.

First discovered by E.H. Hankin in 1896, phages were used successfully by Canadian microbiologist Félix d'Hérelle in Paris in 1917 to treat children with dysentery.[1] Phages are easy to produce, and their use spread. But interest in the West was lost when Fleming discovered penicillin in 1928. In the Eastern bloc, phage therapies continued to be developed and are still used in Georgian hospitals. Bacterial resistance to antibiotics has led to renewed interest in phages in Western medical research.

Antibiotics destroy many of the healthy bacteria in the human diges-tive system, but phages do not. Phages breed rapidly in the human body, while antibiotic levels drop as soon as the medication is introduced into the human body. These factors suggest that phage therapy is *more natural* than antibiotic treatment. That is, phages contrive with rather than against natural phenomena. Thus, their application follows a principle of co-oper-ation with natural phenomena instead of domination. Their use is, accord-ingly I expect, more ecologically sound and therefore more sustainable in the long term.

The success of phage therapy does not mean that all technology not following principles of respect for and co-operation with natural process be immediately abandoned, but that funding priorities could be adjusted to include such principles. People are inventively clever and amazingly resourceful, and there is no reason to believe that scientists who adopt such directives will not make significant advances quickly. The ensuing shift of world view, from an ideology of domination to one of co-operation, would mean real progress. That is, not just specific technical advances, but move-ment toward a praxical conception of nature that is ecologically sound and healthy in the long run for both human beings and the other life forms with which we share the planet. What is needed, given contemporary environmen-tal problems, is a general consciousness-raising concerning nature put to work by policy-makers, scientists, and the ordinary citizens of a growing, globally pervasive, consumer culture.

Other examples already exist of technological practices that are healthy insofar as they respect natural process.[2] For the most part, however, tech-nologies practise a logic of domination with respect to nature—as if nature consists of nothing more than resources available for human appropriation. I suggest, however, that natural phenomena exist for themselves, in their own right and not just for human beings, and that technological intervention is not always superior to natural process.

A Brief History of Science

The idea that natural phenomena are at best passive bodies exploitable by human ingenuity, and at worst enemies to be conquered and overcome, is deeply rooted in the logic and ideology of modern scientific methodology and technological practice. An analysis of Western intellectual history is worryingly reductive, but nonetheless insightful.

In Aristotle's ancient metaphysics, being is substance (*ousia*): formed matter. Things are, first and foremost, matter upon which form has been imposed. Aristotle's account of nature is ambiguous—he first argues in Book II, chapter 1, of *Physics* that *ta physika*, natural entities, are defined by their ability to move, which means for him to grow and develop of their own accord. They are distinct from artifacts (*technê*), which require an agent who selects the appropriate material upon which to impose a preconceived form. Aristotle asks which is more quintessential to nature, form or matter. He answers that form is what makes an entity what it is, and thus, despite his insight that natural entities are fundamentally different from artifacts, insofar as the former are self-developing while the latter are not, he ultimately conceives of natural entities *technologically*. That is to say, Aristotle's metaphysics displace his insight that natural entities are self-developing, a point I will retrieve below for my ecofeminist phenomenology of nature, in favour of a conception in which they too, like artifacts, consist in matter upon which form has been imposed. Nature is thus thought by Aristotle to be a kind of artifact, albeit privileged in that natural things are self-making.

In the subsequent Christian world view, nature is likewise a special kind of artifact, now divinely created. God is the arch-artisan, and furthermore creates the natural world for the sake of his favourite work—human beings. Upon expulsion from the Garden of Eden, Adam is accordingly directed to work the natural world for his own survival and benefit. This promise, that the purpose of nature is to meet human needs, comes to culmination in modern science. Francis Bacon explicitly promises that his new science will harness nature for human benefit (Bacon 1980, 16, 21).

I will not repeat Carolyn Merchant's critique of Bacon's ideology and methodology, but I draw attention to her argument that Baconian science is thoroughly patriarchal, if not downright misogynist. This means that in the intellectual history of the West, the oppression of women is ideologically entwined with the subjugation of nature, a thesis at the heart of ecofeminist thinking. Merchant is not alone in arguing that science and technology have led to environmental disaster. Rachel Carson's *Silent Spring* lays out the catastrophic consequences of technologically based industry, and Vandana Shiva and Val Plumwood argue that such destruction is inherent to the modern scientific world view.

I supplement these analyses with a further point about the mechanistic world view of modern science. When Aristotle said that nature is self-developing, he committed himself to the belief that nature is tecological. He meant that natural entities have a final cause (*telos*), a "for-the-sake-of-which," and that their growth is self-directed to this end. He argued the same explicitly in Book I, chapter 8 of *Physics*. Things in nature do not come about by chance, but rather grow toward an end. Indeed, acorns become neither lions nor swans, for example, but, if they survive and become anything at all, they grow into oak trees. Everything in nature has a goal, a purpose toward which it strives. Modern science contains no such notion of teleology.

One can argue that Newtonian science also is teleological as a way of explaining the action-at-a-distance (accused in his day of being spooky) that Newton calls *vis gravitas*, gravity. But note that his concern here is loco-motion—change of place—not growth, so his metaphysics is, in a sense, static. Nature is for him dead in the way Merchant described. His fantastically successful physics has no place for the insight that natural entities grow toward some end, some purpose of their own. His mechanistic world view lays nature bare for exploitation by eliminating a teleological conception of nature as purposive process. If natural entities are construed as having no inherent purpose, they are rendered available for appropriation toward human purposes. Indeed, the mechanistic world view of modern physics underwrites a patriarchal logic of domination, manifest in technological practices of manipulation and control, applied against natural entities taken to be no more than inert matter, purposeless except insofar as exploited by human intention.

In conjunction with his static metaphysics, Newton has an eye for immortality in his epistemology, which favours the fixed and unchanging. His physics is self-avowedly mathematical.[3] On this basis, Kant secures the truth of modern science in his first *Critique*. The synthetic a priori judgments of physics are true insofar as they are mathematical. Not only is Newton's science ubiquitously calculative, it also follows a geometric method in that he begins with axioms, for example, the law of inertia, on the basis of which he derives further truths. His mathematization of the objects of physics promotes an ideology of immutability against a conception informed by the ongoing motility of nature itself. Human ideas are thus taken to be universally applicable and are granted an authoritative priority over experience. Newton's methodology is empirical insofar as it is experimental, but the function of experiment is primarily verification of a priori hypotheses rather than observation. Everyday experience, the messy realm of the changeable, is no longer the venue of scientific investigation; instead, the scientist works in the idealized, mathematized conditions of the laboratory.

In Newton's physics, then, the unchangeable plays a central role both metaphysically and epistemologically. But do things in the natural world demonstrate such fixity, an immutability that can be described by a priori truths? In his essay, "The Laws of Nature as Habits," Rupert Sheldrake argues that laws of nature are more like habits than truths fixed from the beginning of time, and of course Darwinian evolution suggests the constancy only of change. Nor is nature confined to what is laid out in human ideas—it is full of surprises. Thalidomide, global warming, and SARS provide examples of nature's unpredictability. Aristotle is right: everything in nature is in a constant state of flux, directed by natural teleology.

Perhaps, then, an epistemology that admits of change is more suited to treating natural phenomena. That is, contemporary relations of alienation and abuse between human beings and nature suggest that a new epistemology is called for, one that accepts its own finitude and acknowledges that any world view with respect to nature has its time, flourishes, and then becomes, if not obsolete, certainly no longer the best way to conceive of the natural world. The Baconian-Newtonian paradigm of a mechanistic universe that can be dominated by human knowledge and intention is past its prime in just this way.

Alternative Science

Aristotle's approach provides the beginnings of an alternative. In *Metaphysics* 1.1, Aristotle describes how one comes to know natural phenomena. Through repeated exposure, the universal is stabilized in the soul. Thus one cannot generalize a single incidence universally, as Newton claimed in his fourth rule of reasoning, which states that any quality observed to belong to a body in a single experiment will be taken to hold of all bodies whatsoever. Rather, it is only through repeated experience of things in nature that one comes to see what they are and how they function. Aristotle held that one thereby comes to know the object of enquiry with respect to its universality, but that universality is not grounded in the a priori nature of understanding. Aristotle gave experience priority over theorization in his practice of science. Thus he gave nature, as it were, the first word. Perhaps it is no coincidence that, as a natural scientist, Aristotle was first and foremost a biologist. The most appropriate paradigms for understanding nature may no longer come from physics.

Goethe's practice of science was similar to Aristotle's. His methodology was observational in that he witnessed phenomena in different ways and under different conditions in order to understand what he called the *Ur-*

phenomenon. The latter was not a fixed and static thing, but a metamorphic process. Much as Aristotle held that natural things are in constant motion, Goethe practised a "delicate empiricism" that assumed the wholeness and harmony of nature and learned through extensive and empathetic looking (Goethe 1994, 307). Like Aristotle, he *listened* to what the objects of enquiry told him, rather than reducing and confining them to a priori truths. But Goethe held to his empiricism beyond Aristotle. He refused to leave the phenomenon behind by abstracting to what can be theorized a priori, a move Aristotle accepted once the universal was stabilized in the knower's soul, and advocated instead returning to phenomena again and again. Accordingly, his truths were provisional and always open to revision.

I suggest that such methodological attentiveness can generate an environmentally conscientious science and heal the catastrophic wounds that technological practices have inflicted upon the natural world. First, such science does not give itself the last word, but respects nature's power to exceed human conception and defy prediction. Second, because the science I advocate listens to nature, it cannot help but resist a short-sighted conception of natural entities as fixed and static. This "snapshot" conception of nature can be displaced through acknowledgement that natural beings persist through time, and that they do so in a constant state of flux, change, and adaptability. Both Aristotle and Goethe witnessed in their science nature's teleology, and indeed they were right to do so. Nature *is* teleological, and to recognize and respect natural ends is to be able to work sustainably in conjunction with nature, rather than pursuing a futile dream of subjecting nature to human desire.

"Nature" and Ecofeminist Phenomenology

The term "ecofeminism" was first used in French by Francoise d'Eaubonne in her 1974 book, *Le féminisme ou la mort*. She argued that an excess of reproduction led to the oppression of women, while an excess of production resulted in the exploitation of nature. These two factors combined, she warned, threaten human survival. In response to current problems of species extinction, global climate change, human health hazards arising from ecosystem contamination, and injustices toward humans that have their source in environmental damage and resource depletion, an ecofeminist phenomenology of nature looks for new paradigms of nature and the natural.

What is nature? "Nature" and "natural" are slippery words that have had and continue to have a plethora of diverse and divergent meanings. The words come to English via French from the Latin *natura*, which is derived from the Greek *nasci*, meaning to be born, originate, grow, be produced. The earliest use of nature in written English occurred in a sermon in 1250 describing the "nature of man."[4] Nature thus originally meant a thing's nature (Dryden first used the expression "human nature" in 1668), that is, its essential properties and capacities, and the impulse that drives its action. For example, nature was commonly said to impel defecation and urination, a usage that appears to have become obsolete after the eighteenth century (though in Alberta and perhaps elsewhere, a person heading for the toilet still says "Nature calls!" especially at a bush party).

By the late fourteenth century, nature had become a thing in its own right, and Chaucer personified nature as "she" in his *Canterbury Tales*: "she pricks the birds into singing." Originally, natural offspring meant not illegitimate. Today, who is the natural mother—the birth mother or she who provides the egg? Ironically, no one was said to be born by natural childbirth until 1933, though someone was first described as dying of natural causes in 1576. Law could be natural as early as the 1300s, but rights were not natural until the eighteenth century. In the sixteenth century, a natural was a half-wit, but by the twentieth century, to be a natural was to be particularly clever at doing something. In the 1600s, certain numbers, logarithms, and sines became natural, as did musical notes that were not flat or sharp. In the 1700s, harmonies and instruments could be natural. Physicists used to be called natural philosophers, and the term natural scientist first appeared in 1885. In the 1900s, natural deduction is found in logic, and natural selection in evolutionary theory. Nature conservation appeared in 1949 and natural resources in 1956. Over the centuries, certain kinds of magic (1477), medical skill or treatment (1597), religion (1675), and theology (1677) have all been called natural. One can get a natural when playing cards (1762) or dice (1897).

Evidently, nature and natural are fantastically broad of scope and can be applied to things that do not appear natural at all, like numbers and musical instruments. Some uses are contradictory, as with the idiot versus the gifted. Often, something is not called natural until there is an obvious contrast; for example, natural childbirth makes sense once pharmaceuticals are an option. Indeed, nature and natural have often been understood by way of contrast, especially against what is divine or miraculous, and what is technological, manufactured, or artificial. Witness the following phrases: in one's pure naturals (1579, meaning naked), and a natural wig (1724, meaning made of real hair!). Shakespeare was, in *The Tempest*, the first to contrast nature and nurture. Nature has often been understood not on its own terms, but negatively, in terms of what it is not. What is natural is not synthetic, not socially constructed, and not a product of human civilization. Positive accounts also fail to conceive nature on its own terms, but impose a human idea. In the ideology of science, nature appears as object, nothing more than passive matter that can be harnessed toward human ends, which application reduces nature to mere resource.

I suggest an alternative eco-logic, that is, a different way of thinking about nature, one that acknowledges its multiplicity, adaptability, and motility of meaning. Nature is an ongoing, cyclical, yet ever-changing, self-directed process. As far as human understanding goes, there can be no all-encompassing architectonic, because knowledge is situated, limited, finite, and perspectival, and, mirroring nature, can grow, change, and adapt. Nature is *that which always exceeds any interpretation.*

This view is ecofeminist in that it accepts the ecofeminist criticism that the history of the West plays out a patriarchal logic of domination, and that this logic is at the heart of modern science and technology. In addition, it rejects patriarchal notions of authority and control over the natural world, and favours instead a discourse of home, care, co-operation, and interrelation. It has no pretensions to eternal truth, but is anti-reductionist. It is tentative and open to revision. I invite criticism because this phenomenology insists that it too is subject to a "law of the provisional," and is itself always on the way. That does not mean that I have not thought out the view carefully, but rather that I respect my own ability to change through learning. I advocate conceptions of nature that model the organic: they are born, have their time, grow old, and decay. They are world-based, and their cultural and historical contextualization makes them always open to question, particularly questions of environmental justice. Truths outlive their use, or become like a senile king whose continuing rule ruins what was once a thriving empire. The Baconian-Newtonian paradigm of nature as inert object to be mastered is one such waning ideology that no longer serves to promote human interests or ecological health, and now underwrites catastrophic practices of destruction. Newtonian science has a place in human practice, but can be tempered by insights into natural teleology, so that a balance might be restored in which technological practices respect and work in accord with natural process.

Furthermore, this phenomenology is ecofeminist in that it respects indigenous lifestyles and traditional practices rather than trivializing local knowledge as old wives' tales. In fact, I recommend that indigenous ways of doing things, which characteristically respect the role of natural phenomena in local ecology, be sought out and valued as age-old wisdom from which Western scientists and technologists can learn. I welcome ecofeminist spiritualities because they contain ways of knowing that are alternative to Western scientific paradigms. True to ecofeminist respect for diversity, this phenomenology is both metaphysically and epistemologically pluralist. It is not threatened by differences of opinion but welcomes them in order to nurture conversation among many voices. And it promotes ecofeminist ethics of care toward the self and other humans and non-humans.

This philosophy is phenomenological because I advocate an openness to natural phenomena; that is, listening to and observing them rather than expecting all things in nature to conform to a priori human conceptions. Goethe's science, for example, is phenomenological insofar as it favours phenomena over ideas.[5] His methodology was to remain open to natural phenomena, to follow along behind them attentively observing instead of leading them according to an idea. To put it bluntly, rocks talk and I recommend listening to them rather than imposing categories of understanding.[6] Nature is neither mere scientific object nor mere resource for technological appropriation, but the fundamental moment of the life world. It is home, regardless of how alienated we may have become from that home; it is where people live, not just where eco-tourists take vacations. Human being is part of nature, a player, not an overlord. Modern technology may conduce the delusion that human being has extricated itself from the natural world, but we remain natural beings who must suffer sickness, sleep, eat, go to the toilet, grow old, and pass away. No matter how much human being modifies its world and surrounds itself by technology, nature is fundamental to all lived experience.

On a more personal, concluding note, my son was born five weeks early, so he was immediately whisked away by an obstetrics team. The doctor, herself five months pregnant, had pushed for a Caesarian. She said she didn't trust vaginal delivery. Nonetheless, I delivered in five hours with no surgical or pharmaceutical intervention. I had a slight fever, so too did he. But because he was not lying against my body, he was unable to sustain his body temperature and was moved to intensive care, where he was put under lights for mild jaundice. I wasn't allowed to work with natural process by taking him into sunshine to counteract the jaundice (a much pleasanter experience for us both!), as that meant entering a public area where he might catch something, and interrupting the intravenous drip he was given to counteract dehydration by the lights. Some intervention made more intervention necessary. Despite the lights, his jaundice-level increased, flattened on the fourth day, and then dropped, exactly according to the normal pattern of jaundice in preemies, so it is hard to believe that the technologists were in control of the process.

I do not suggest that medical science does not achieve miracles in sustaining premature life, that no birth requires medical intervention, or that the nurses were not wonderful. They were excellent at their jobs and were simply following hospital policy and standard procedure. I tell this story, rather, as anecdotal evidence of a disrespect for natural process in science in general, and in the medical industry in this particular case. My son's jaundice was treated like an enemy to be conquered. Rather, it was a natural phenomenon that could be trusted to right itself, which is exactly what it appears to have done.

Now he is five months old. He is content to lie on a blanket and watch the wind in the trees above him for ages, with a concentration I would never have expected of such a small person. Though given to maternal anticipations of brilliance, I attribute his attention span to the fact that he is at home in nature. He talks to the wind and the trees in his own language. When the wind drops and the branches stop moving, he kicks his feet, waves his tiny fists, and shouts, as if demanding that the movement return. I smile that he thinks it's in his power to control the wind, and shake my head, "You'll learn." Yet after hundreds of years, modern science and technology are only now beginning to mature to the insight that nature does not succumb to human will, that things in nature are on their own journey.

…At last, I close the computer and collect my son so we can go together and look at a tree. That's what our eyes are made for.

Notes

1 The facts given here about the history of phages are taken from John MacGregor, "Set a bug to catch a bug," *New Scientist* 178, 2389 (April 5, 2003): 36.
2 I have drawn examples from agriculture, oilfield restoration, and flowform technology in Trish Glazebrook, "Art or Nature? Aristotle, Restoration Ecology, and Flowforms," *Ethics and Environment* 8, 1 (2003): 22–36.
3 H.S. Thayer, ed., *Newton's Philosophy of Nature: Selections from His Writings* (New York: Hafner Press, 1953).
4 The word must have already been in conversational use, but it first appeared in writing when sermons began to be delivered in the vernacular. This instance and the following history of usage are taken from the *Oxford English Dictionary*.
5 See David Seamon and Arthur Zajonc, eds., *Goethe's Way of Science: A Phenomenology of Nature* (Albany: State University of New York Press, 1998) for further arguments that Goethe's science is phenomenological.

6 Cf. Christine Turner, "Messages in Stone: Field Geology in the American West," in *Earth Matters: The Earth Sciences, Philosophy, and the Claims of Community*, ed. Robert Frodeman (Upper Saddle River, NJ: Prentice-Hall, 2000), 51–62. Turner is a geologist with the United States Geological Survey who argues that rocks talk.

Works Cited

Aristotle. *Physics, Books I–IV*. Trans. P.H. Wicksteed and F.M. Cornford. Cambridge, MA: Harvard University Press, 1929.

———. *Metaphysics I–IX*. Trans. Hugh Tredennick. Cambridge, MA: Harvard University Press, 1933.

Bacon, Francis. *The Great Instauration and New Atlantis*. Ed. J. Weinburger. Arlington Heights, IL: Harlan Davidson, 1980.

Carson, Rachel. *Silent Spring*. Boston: Houghton Mifflin, 1962.

d'Eaubonne, Françoise. *Le Feminisme ou La Mort*. Paris: Pierre Horay, 1974.

Goethe, J.W. von. *Goethe: Scientific Studies*. Trans. D. Miller. Princeton, NJ: Princeton University Press, 1944.

Kant, Immanuel. *Critique of Pure Reason*. Trans. Norman Kemp Smith. London: Macmillan, 1929.

Merchant, Carolyn. *The Death of Nature: Women, Ecology, and the Scientific Revolution*. San Francisco: Harper & Row, 1980.

Ondaatje, Michael. *The English Patient*. New York: Knopf, 1992.

Plumwood, Val. *Feminism and the Mastery of Nature*. London: Routledge, 1993.

Shakespeare, William. *The Tempest*. London: Methuen, 1962.

Sheldrake, Rupert, "The Laws of Nature as Habits." In *The Reenchantment of Science*, ed. David Ray Griffin. Albany, NY: State University of New York Press, 1988.

Shiva, Vandana. *Staying Alive: Women, Ecology, and Development*. London: Zed Books, 1988.

9

Romantic Origins of Environmentalism

Wordsworth and Shelley

Onno Oerlemans

The past twenty years have seen a burgeoning of criticism arguing that Romanticism is an important origin for contemporary attitudes towards the natural world.[1] It is not a surprising development. We can easily see that the works of particular European and American writers in the late-eighteenth and early-nineteenth centuries reflect a marked change in ideas about nature. Before this period, Judeo-Christian culture held that humankind was very much at the centre of the universe, given this sacrosanct place by God himself. As Lynn White has influentially argued, the creation narrative of Genesis firmly represents the belief that nature exists for our purposes (1967, 1203–207). It made sense, then, as Newton and Descartes argued, that the natural world—from the solar system to animals—was a more or less mechanistic realm, completely devoid of and separate from the divine soul, which humans alone shared with God. Romantic-period thinkers changed and complicated this world view in a number of ways. First, they came to think of nature as organic rather than mechanistic, which is to say that they felt that the natural world was itself growing and changing, rather than fixed like clockwork simply to provide a temporary place for our existence. This idea was supported by scientific insight into biology and geology which showed that specific systems were themselves dynamic rather than static, and that the world was vastly older than the biblical account of creation allowed. Second, the place of humankind within the natural world was dramatically altered, in often vexed ways.

Rather than being figuratively at the centre of nature's purpose, and at the top of the natural chain of being, humans came to seem increasingly connected to this new, dynamic, natural world. We were part of nature's purpose, which turns out to be far more inscrutable than that of God. We were also a kind of stepchild to nature, increasingly aware of nature's indifference to our existence, and of our actual and paradoxical separation from nature through our self-conscious ability to reflect on our place within it.

These ideas, we will see, are part of the fabric of Romantic thought, evident in the scientific writings of Erasmus Darwin and Gilbert White, and the poetry of Wordsworth, Coleridge, Shelley, and Clare.[2] Part of the importance of Romanticism is precisely the influence it had on later environmental thinkers and writers. Its environmental legacy extends through Emerson and Thoreau, who are the crucial influences on American environmental writers, from John Muir and Aldo Leopold to Barry Lopez and Annie Dillard, and in England through John Ruskin and William Morris.[3] There is another curious legacy of Romanticism within environmentalism, however. We can detect this legacy when we hear the frequent accusation that environmentalist beliefs and ideals are merely "romantic." The word used in this context suggests (as it did during the actual Romantic period, 1790–1830) ideas that are idealistic, naive, fanciful, unscientific, and irrational. Romantic-period writing, especially in contrast to that of the Enlightenment, can seem all these things; the Romantic poets largely did celebrate imagination over reason and idealism over pragmatism. More importantly for our purposes, they were also accused of heresy and solipsism for their ability to project versions of their own consciousness onto landscape in an attempt to recover an immanent deity. That is, the unity and connection they attempted to make with the natural world can appear as little more than a projection of their own desires and emotions.

Indeed, this is the charge made in a recent essay by an important environmentalist writer who attempts to rescue contemporary environmentalism from its current and past Romanticism. William Cronon argues that Romantic-period writers are responsible for a deep and long-lasting refiguring of the idea of nature as a pristine wilderness. Attempting to show that wilderness is "quite profoundly a human creation" (1996, 69), he argues that Romanticism transformed our idea about the natural world into a kind of sanctuary, removed from and opposed to human culture and civilization. In a pointedly reductive argument, Cronon suggests that writers like Burke and Wordsworth are responsible for making nature that place so removed from human contamination that we might again find God there. The Romantic project, he argues, is an attempt to secularize God, removing Him from human artifacts like cathedrals to the natural world, and thereby transforming wilderness as a cultural idea from something barren and terrifying into "those rare places on earth where one had more chance than elsewhere to glimpse the face of God" (1996, 73). Cronon's ultimate point is that, instructed by the Romantics and their heirs, we continue to idealize nature, constructing an idea of it as existing only in pristine, untouched environments, the illogical outcome of which is to demand our own removal from the landscape in order to purify it. Nature, Cronon wants to argue, is everywhere, and we are part of it.

While Cronon's goal of expanding the current popular understanding of what is natural is laudable, it rests upon a revealing and enduring simplification of Romanticism. This simplification sees a part for the whole. In Emerson's great transparent eyeball passage from his essay "Nature," in which he depicts himself stepping out of culture into the 'other' of the natural world in an attempt to define original relation to the universe, we can see a key example of the kind of Romanticism that Cronon focuses on. The natural world is used by Emerson as a way of isolating the self from culture, so that the God that is discovered here is, in a profound sense, the autonomous self, the individual who seems able to remove himself from history and culture.[4] This is indeed a central trope of Romanticism, powerfully depicted in Emerson's career. But Romanticism, and Romantic-period writers, are more complex than just this example suggests. Specifically, their encounters with the natural world, the meaning they take from it, their investigations of it, their needs for it simply are not adequately summarized by Emerson's famous example, or by the similar ones Cronon presents.

I want in this essay to examine two other paradigmatic moments that, in their opposition to each other, reveal more clearly Romanticism's complex and sometimes contradictory attitudes to the natural world. My examples are Wordsworth's "Lines: Written a Few Miles Above Tintern Abbey" (commonly referred to as "Tintern Abbey," even though this landmark does not figure in the poem), and Shelley's "Mont Blanc."[5] The two poems are absolutely central to the Romantic canon—each clearly represents a seminal moment in its author's poetic development, and each has had enormous influence in the histories of poetry and thinking about the natural world. Moreover, Shelley's poem is itself a response to "Tintern Abbey," explicitly conceived as a modification to an attitude that the poet nevertheless felt had tremendous influence on him. I will not offer comprehensive interpretations of these two much studied and analyzed poems, but rather highlight the manner in which they reveal complex, central, and opposed under-standings of the natural world. My aim is to show simultaneously that Romantic-period writing has had an enduring effect on the way we look at the natural world, and that its influences are not easily reducible to a sin-gle impulse.

My "green" reading of "Tintern Abbey" focuses not simply on how nature in the poem is shown to be restorative, ameliorating the poet's moral and imaginative decline, but also on how this process is attributed to a pro-found interconnection between consciousness and the physical world. Typ-ically for Wordsworth, the scene that the poet has returned to after "the length / Of five long winters" is not a particularly "wild" place. It is not sub-lime, striking the speaker with awe and fear, but is pastoral and picturesque, characterized by a beautiful and seemingly controlled irregularity. Indeed, its effect on the speaker has less to do with extraordinary intrinsic features of the setting than with the speaker's own familiarity with it; it is a place that already made an impression on his consciousness five years before. The poem highlights the degree to which the speaker is making use of the moment, and the place, to take stock of his own imaginative growth, and ulti-mately to proffer a theory that the imagination is most vibrant, healthy, and moral when it is intimately familiar with the natural world. The first verse paragraph, for instance, opens with the urgency of the poet being at this particular spot on the Banks of the Wye, "a few miles above Tintern Abbey," when he can "once again ... repose / Here, under this dark sycamore." His familiarity with the spot enables him explicitly to mould it in his imagina-tion for his own purpose. Needing a place of "deep seclusion," he is able to push to the background, but not eliminate, evidence of human activity on the landscape. "Plots of cottage ground ... / Among the woods and copses lose themselves," while "hedge-rows" become "hardly hedge-rows, little lines/ Of sportive wood run wild." The poet's imagination, fueled by his desire to be secluded, makes everything a part of "the wild green landscape." He has created a virtual Eden whose explicit purpose, as we find out it in the next section, is solace and comfort.

The poem's remarkable argument has already been introduced by exam-ple: that viewing rural, relatively natural landscape, makes one better, not just in the negative sense of providing an escape from one's individual and cultural past, but in a direct and positive way by making one more percep-tive, imaginative, and moral. Wordsworth's poem thus articulates what is a deep and often unspoken tenet of much environmental thought (one that may be found in virtually all the great nature writers, from Thoreau and

Muir to Dillard, Mowat, and Lopez). The rest of the poem provides a number of complementing explanations for how a connection to the natural world has sustained the poet's faith in himself. The scene just described is a synecdoche for nature in its entirety and the poet's memories of his many connections with it. The poem is thus a miniature of *The Prelude*, which Wordsworth would begin a year later, an autobiography that details the many different places and times that he had similar experiences. Abstractly, the poet is concerned with documenting how the natural world's "forms of beauty" have made him who he is. The autobiographical moment of this poem is in fact the subject of intense and sustained critical debate, but the poem itself (like the beginning of *The Prelude*) suggests a crucial turning point, a return to the familiarity of natural beauty after five long years of uncertainty, characterized by "the din / Of towns and cities," and perhaps also the complex moral crisis associated with Wordsworth's dashed sympathies with the French Revolution (hinted at in dating the poem's meditation as occurring on the eve of Bastille Day).[6]

The poem's importance, historically and in terms of our green reading of it, lies most of all with the psychological interpretation of the effects of these "forms of beauty." That the natural world can be a pleasant and restorative place had long been a central trope of poetry, particularly that of the pastoral and georgic traditions. Wordsworth, however, aims to make this trope a literal truth. Thus the poem's second section argues that simply remembering nature's beauty, and the sensations one had in first perceiving it, can provide "tranquil restoration." More than this, though, the poet argues that these sensations become "felt in the blood, and felt along the heart," and thus become seemingly oxymoronic "feelings ... of unremembered pleasure." This is really the heart of the poem's argument, and it is given abstractly in the poem's second section: that the sensations of pleasure one has in the presence of natural beauty are more than simply moments of experience which can be recalled with pleasure; they become as well a part of one's being, so that one has literally "taken in" an aspect of the external world. Much of the poem describes how this process of taking in nature's influence occurs, while the poem's first thirty lines or so recount the impetus of the poet's need to recognize that nature's beauty is already a part of his being.

The other "gift" of nature this section describes is perception, as achieved in a "blessed mood" created and guided by beauty itself:

> In which the affections gently lead us on,
> Until, the breath of this corporeal frame,
> And even the motion of our human blood

> Almost suspended, we are laid asleep
> In body, and become a living soul:
> While with an eye made quiet by the power
> Of harmony, and the deep power of joy,
> We see into the life of things.

This is clearly a key source for both Emerson's and Thoreau's notions of transcendence. It is an abstract summary of what has already happened in the meditation that the poem represents, most clearly in the poem's first section. The mental state described here is a fine balance between activity and passivity, between urgently taking in the external forms of beauty and of quietly responding to the beauty that is unquestionably out there. What is produced by these moments of perception is a conviction that the beauty, harmony, and power the poet perceives are both genuinely there, of the world, and the result of an imagination already nurtured by these aspects of nature. The former is a guarantee of a larger, generally benign spirit of the natural world—its being—while the latter is for Wordsworth the essential requirement for being a poet.

Yet the poet allows for doubt about both these convictions: "If this / Be but a vain belief…." The two final sections of the poem attempt to reconstruct and reaffirm this belief from two different vantage points: the first by reassessing the "picture of the mind" through a highly condensed story of the growth of his own consciousness, and the second, and more problematic, by seeing signs of both the "blessed mood" and of the poet's former self in his sister, whom we learn in the final section is actually the immediate audience for the entire utterance of the poem. The autobiography focuses on what the poet perceives as the key change in how he responds to nature in the present, as opposed to "when first / I came among these hills." In these earlier years, his response to natural splendor was relatively intense and spontaneous, "an appetite: a feeling and a love, / That had no need of a remoter charm, / By thought supplied." Now, however, he must seek out this beauty, and make a deliberate and conscious effort (as he does in the opening section of the poem) to see and appreciate it. This loss of spontaneity means the end of the "aching joys" and "dizzy raptures" of being in the natural world. However, the "abundant recompense" for these losses, the poet argues, is precisely the ability to bring thought to this process of perception, developing a deeper harmony between self and nature.

> For I have learned
> To look on nature, not as in the hour

Of thoughtless youth, but hearing oftentimes
The still, sad music of humanity,
Nor harsh nor grating, though of ample power
To chasten and subdue. And I have felt
A presence that disturbs me with the joy
Of elevated thoughts, a sense sublime
Of something far more deeply interfused,
Whose dwelling is the light of setting suns,
And the round ocean, and the living air,
And the blue sky, and in the mind of man,
A motion and a spirit, that impels
All thinking things, all objects of all thought,
And rolls through all things.

There is no doubt that this is a mystical experience. The poet suggests the existence, quite literally, of a "spirit of nature," a consciousness which includes all things, and of which our own consciousness is but a small part. Thus, when we look at the natural world most profoundly we see and hear ourselves, not at its centre, but as "still" and "sad," because though we are a part of it, we are also estranged from it. This is a lucid and beautiful rendering of the idea that is now at the centre of much of "deep ecology," which stresses the need to recognize the natural world not as objective and "other" than our consciousness, but as itself inter-subjective, an idea figured in popular culture both in the cliche of "mother nature," and in the Gaia hypothesis, which holds that the entire biotic community functions as a single organism.[7] Wordsworth would in fact never be entirely comfortable with the pantheism he implies with "Tintern Abbey," and his many vacillations on the rendering of the idea of the spirit of nature have been one of the enduring topics of literary criticism of the Romantic period.[8] What a green reading of the poem can fruitfully emphasize, however, is that perceiving nature as directly and openly as possible has the effect of making us more fully human, and forces us to recognize the degree to which consciousness is dependent upon the natural world. Another way of saying this is that Wordsworth here (as in *The Prelude* and even more explicitly in *Home at Grasmere*) argues that the natural world is imagination's natural home. This is not yet an idea about the need for preserving the natural world, or understanding a natural economy in biological terms, but it is a fundamental step in developing a sense of why the natural world matters to us as something other than a source of raw material. It gives nature a value beyond the merely instrumental.

Wordsworth's poem is thus a fine statement about an ideal of harmony and likeness between humankind and the natural world, and this idea particularly is often seen as lying at the heart of Romanticism's reconception of nature. But this is not the whole story, for in Shelley's "Mont Blanc" we have an example of a radically different view of the natural world, and one that is equally fundamental to current environmental thinking: it is that the natural world is defined by its materiality, and that this physical "otherness" is profoundly inaccessible to, and different from, consciousness.

The poem's brilliant opening metaphor makes this point viscerally, while playing off the most famous lines of "Tintern Abbey." The speaker of this poem too is meditating on the meaning of a particular place, but here consciousness is overwhelmed by the sheer physical presence of the external world. For Shelley, there is no possibility of sharing some element of consciousness with the spectacular mountain he is confronting. Instead, "the everlasting universe of things / Flows through the mind," drowning out, as the elaborate metaphor continues to dramatize, whatever it is that "human thought" can bring to such a place, just as the sound of a secret spring is overwhelmed in

> the wild woods, among the mountains lone,
> Where waterfalls around it leap for ever,
> Where woods and winds contend, and a vast river
> Over its rocks ceaselessly bursts and raves.

There is a fine irony here, at Wordsworth's expense, in suggesting that human thought in such an environment "assumes...a sound but half its own." The point is that human thought is essentially annihilated in this place, so that it is clearly an error to assume that what races through consciousness in the act of perceiving the spectacle of such a large and seemingly wild mountain is anything other than the physical universe itself.

The poem is an extended and precise description of the mountain scene, loosely organized around the gradual ascent of the speaker's gaze along the Ravine of Arve, the slopes of Mont Blanc (then as now the most famous and dramatically "scenic" of the many peaks of the Alps) to its summit. Like Wordsworth, Shelley is trying to understand the relationship between the physical universe, at Mont Blanc seemingly revealed in its most naked form, and human consciousness and culture. What does it mean, the poet repeatedly asks, that the natural world is in fact monstrously indifferent and even hostile to human activity and thought? What does it mean that in the natural world even something so obvious and striking as Mont Blanc cannot reveal its meaning? The brilliance of the poem lies in part in Shelley's ability to contrast the act of perceiving the mountain to the infinitude of the physical universe. The poem's second section, for instance, is another ironic echoing of "Tintern Abbey"; whereas Wordsworth is able to recreate a single and seemingly unified and meaningful picture from his immediate environment, the speaker in "Mont Blanc" is clearly overwhelmed by the sheer size and variety of what he sees. The meaning here is not of the possibility of a peaceful seclusion, abetted by a comfortingly pastoral space, but is of that which refuses to reveal itself (like the "waterfall, whose veil/ Robes some unsculptured image"). Thus the speaker is left

> To muse on my own separate fantasy,
> My own my human mind, which passively
> Now renders and receives fast influencings,
> Holding an unremitting interchange
> With the clear universe of things around;
> One legion of wild thoughts, whose wandering wings
> Now float above thy darkness....

Consciousness is made to seem unreal next to what we might call the ultra-reality of the mountain, its glaciers, and the ravine which comes down from them. Its images pass rapidly through the mind as it attempts helplessly to fashion them, through the words of the poem, into something coherent. "The spirit fails," the poet repeats in the next section, because what coherence there is speaks of the absolute permanence and otherness of this physical reality, and the utter insignificance not just of human thought but of human existence in general. Thus the mountain is characterized by "unearthly forms," "unfathomable deeps," and

> A desert peopled by the storms alone,
> Save when the eagle brings some hunter's bone,
> And the wolf tracks her there.

The mountain speaks of a natural world that is relentlessly carnivorous and predatory, an especially horrific realization for the deeply vegetarian poet. It is, indeed, a "city of death/a flood of ruin." The glaciers and screes seem to the poet a testament to nature's deepest cycles of destruction and renewal. Indeed, Shelley refers here to the new geological science which was just beginning to reveal that the earth must in fact be millions of years old, rather than the few thousand years told of in the Bible.[9] This deep history of the earth seems to Shelley to shatter utterly humankind's claim to sit atop the chain of being, to be at the centre, somehow, of the universe. The "power" of Mont Blanc overwhelms not just individual consciousness, but also the seeming privilege and progress of human history.

> The rocks, drawn down
> From yon remotest waste, have overthrown
> The limits of the dead and living world,
> Never to be reclaimed. The dwelling-place
> Of insects, beasts, and birds, becomes its spoil
> Their food and their retreat for ever gone,
> So much of life and joy is lost. The race
> Of man flies far in dread; his work and dwelling
> Vanish, like smoke before the tempest's stream,
> And their place is not known.

In spite of this vision of destruction and death, the speaker stresses throughout that he is being taught by this scene, that a powerful truth—"the secret Strength of things/Which governs thought, and to the infinite dome/Of heaven is as a law"—has been revealed to him. The climax of the poem occurs at the end of section III, when the speaker announces that, "Thou hast a voice, great Mountain, to repeal/Large codes of fraud and woe, not understood/By all." This is an astonishing claim, for in one sense it is hard to imagine how a vision of the infinite power and strength of the natural world as it is presented in the poem can do anything other than make us feel helpless and pathetic. Yet Shelley is entirely serious here, even though he is thematically echoing Wordsworth, who also claims that gazing at the natural world can make us better people. The "mysterious tongue" of nature in this poem, though, teaches an "awful doubt" rather than Wordsworth's "faith so mild." Shelley argues in part for the efficacy of a radical skepticism, a sense that in contrast to the deep necessity of the natural world (its hidden laws), human laws are temporary, artificial, and probably wrong, and thus (as Shelley argues in many other of his major poems) may be challenged and changed.

The two poems I've examined present very distinct poles in Romantic thinking about the natural world. Wordsworth's poem depicts a deep desire to establish a nearly physical link between our consciousness and the external realm, a sense in which we are all part of one "spirit." It suggests a desire, too, to overcome our traditional assumption that we are unproblematically at the centre of God's plan for nature, that it has been designed for us, and that we are somehow nature's supreme creation (all versions of anthropocentrism). Wordsworth's view lends itself to a kind of natural egalitarianism. Indeed, one of the direct consequences of the poet's search for common spirit in nature is, as I have argued elsewhere, the ability to see animal life as other important "modes of being," tangible evidence of the spirit of nature.[10] In Shelley's view, on the other hand, the physical world is inimical to consciousness. It remains profoundly "other" and inaccessible. Shelley's view is far more radically anti-anthropocentric; that is, in "Mont Blanc" humanity is clearly shaken from its assumptions of self-importance in the natural world. Not only is the natural world not merely instrumental for our purposes, we are not even instrumental for whatever we might take to be its designs. If Wordsworth allows that nature is familiar and harmonious because it contains, and is perhaps a projection of, our desires, Shelley argues that nature is pure matter and thus completely resistant to such desire. Shelley's view is consistent with a more materialistic and scientifically driven understanding of our relationship to the natural world, which views nature in terms of the complex systems of ecology, evolution, and geology. Shelley, like this strain of contemporary environmental thought, is much more hesitant about defining what our relationship to these systems is, except to say that we are inescapably a part of them.

In arguing against the reductionism of Cronon's view of Romanticism and its effect on the development of environmental thought, I have been guilty of simplifications as well. The poles of thought I have presented here as existing between Wordsworth and Shelley also occur within the works of both these poets. In other poems, Wordsworth also reveals a skepticism of his own anthropomorphism, and an awareness of the fundamental differences between the physical world and consciousness. So, too, Shelley in other works envisions tranquil, positively utopian, understandings of human spirit in profound harmony with natural laws and spirits. Moreover, there are many other aspects of "green Romanticism," that do not fit easily into the vision of either of the two poems I've examined—such as Coleridge's, Wordsworth's, and Clare's evocations of animal consciousness and animal rights, the complex cross-influencing of Romantic-period sciences and literature, and the beginnings of a more pragmatic ethic and science for actually living in, and recreating, our environments (from picturesque landscaping to kinds of "green" architecture). Nonetheless, the antithesis presented by the two poems I've examined here has been central in the development of environmental thinking. Contemporary environmentalism also vacillates between thinking of nature as our benign and spiritual home, and as a complex network of physical systems we only partially understand, which in themselves teach us nothing about how we are to define our proper relationship with the natural world.

Notes

1   Important texts include: Jonathan Bate, *Romantic Ecology* (London: Routledge, 1991); Lawrence Buell, *The Environmental Imagination* (Cambridge, MA: Belknap, 1995); and Karl Kroeber, *Ecological Literary Criticism: Romantic Imagining and the Biology of Mind* (New York: Columbia University Press, 1994).

2   Eramus Darwin, grandfather of Charles Darwin, was a natural historian and published a number of long poems that contained his vision of how the natural world worked. See particularly, *The Loves of Plants* (London: J. Johnson, 1789) and *Zoonomia, or the Laws of Organic Life* (London: J. Johnson, 1796). Gilbert White's *The Natural History and Antiquities of Selborne* (London: T. Bensley, 1789) was a very popular work of amateur natural history, recording his meticulous observations of the natural world around him. Samuel Taylor Coleridge published a number of well-known poems on the natural world (including "The Rime of the Ancient Mariner") and wrote as well a philosophical treatise called *The Theory of Life* [in *Shorter Works and Fragments*, H.J. Jackson and J.R. de J. Jackson, eds., vol. 11 of *The Collected Works of Samuel Taylor Coleridge* (Princeton: Princeton University Press, 1995)] which attempted to find the key idea of the organization of all life.) John Clare was a relatively uneducated "peasant-poet" who wrote dozens of poems reflecting his keen observation of the natural world around him.

3   Emerson's essay *Nature* (Boston: Beacon Press, 1985) and Thoreau's book *Walden* (Boston: Houghton Mifflin, 1960) are the key examples here. The most important book on the legacy of Thoreau and Emerson in American environmental writing is *The Environmental Imagination* by Lawrence Buell. Jonathan Bate's *Romantic Ecology* suggests the influence of Romantic thought on Ruskin's thinking about the natural world, particularly in *Unto This Last* (New York: Penguin, 1985). Wordsworth's influence is evident in William Morris's *News from Nowhere* (New York: Cambridge University Press, 1995) as well, in its imagining of a rural utopia.

4   This criticism of "Romantic ideology" was a cornerstone of literary criticism of the 1980s and early 1990s. See particularly, Jerome McGann, *The Romantic Ideology* (Chicago: University of Chicago Press, 1983); Alan Liu, *Wordsworth: The Sense of History* (Stanford: Stanford University Press, 1989); and David Simpson, *Wordsworth's Historical Imagination* (London: Methuen, 1987).

5   I have taken the text of both poems from the excellent anthology *British Literature, 1780–1830*, Anne Mellor and Richard Matlack, eds. (New York: Harcourt Brace, 1996).

6   See especially Marjorie Levinson's reading of the poem in *Wordsworth's Great Period Poems* (New York: Cambridge University Press, 1986). She argues that by reconstructing details of what Wordsworth might actually have been seeing, "we can tell that he was deliberately distorting the scene in order to assert the power of his imagination" (24). Articles supporting and refuting Levinson's claim are too numerous to list here.

7 On deep ecology, see Arne Naess, *Ecology, Community and Lifestyle*, trans. and rev. by David Rothenberg (New York: Cambridge University Press, 1989). On Gaia, see James Lovelock, *Gaia: A New Look at Life on Earth* (New York: Oxford University Press, 1987).

8 In the "Intimations" ode, for instance, Wordsworth uses the Platonic idea that "Our birth is but a sleep and a forgetting"; that is, that our soul comes from some larger spirit and forgets this origin when it is born. In other poems, and especially in later revisions of early poems, Wordsworth increasingly refers to the spirit or consciousness that he perceives in the natural world as God. Coleridge, with whom Wordsworth worked closely early in their careers, shows a similar vacillation in his poetry. The heavily revised poem "The Aeolian Harp" (first published as "Effusion xxxv") presents the poet's speculation on the existence of "one intellectual Breeze. At once the Soul of each and God of all." In "Dejection: An Ode," however, written just six years later and in direct opposition to Wordsworth's more hopeful belief, Coleridge argues that "we receive but what we give,/And in our life alone does Nature live." In this poem, Coleridge presents nature as "inanimate," and whatever spirit and meaning we find in it is a projection of our own imaginative power.

9 The revolution in geology was brought about in part by James Hutton's *Theory of the Earth* (Edinburgh: W. Creech, 1795), which argued for the slow and gradual transformation of earth's surface. Hutton's insights clearly implied that the earth must be at least millions of years old.

10 Onno Oerlemans, "The Meanest Thing That Feels: Anthropomorphizing Animals in Romanticism," *Mosaic* 27 (1994): 1–32.

Works Cited

Cronon, William. "The Trouble with Wilderness; or, Getting Back to the Wrong Nature." In *Uncommon Ground*, ed. William Cronon. New York: W.W. Norton, 1996.

White Jr., Lynn. "The Historical Roots of Our Ecological Crisis," *Science* 155 (1967): 1203–207.

10

Wintergreen: Reflections from Loon Lake
Afterword
Monte Hummel

Aldo Leopold originally wrote *A Sand County Almanac* under the working title "Great Possessions." Among my greatest "possessions" at Loon Lake are the thick beds of wintergreen plants that carpet the forest floor year-round. Even the phrase "wintergreen" is evocative of the Canadian landscape, seasons, and character. This self-reliant little plant doesn't just endure winter; it relishes it.

With its rich, dark green, leathery leaves and bright red berries, both of which it maintains even under the snow, wintergreen (*Gaultheria procumbens*) is one of Canada's best-known wild plants. A member of the health family, it has at least twenty-five common or local names. In his 1939 book, *Edible Wild Plants*, Oliver Perry Medsger wrote, "No other wild plant led [me] into the woods so often as this one. Its mere name recalls many pleasant rambles afield for the leaves and berries" (67).

Wintergreen grows three to six inches (7 to 15 cm) high on upright branches from a more extensive system of creeping or underground stems. This invisible, interconnected network which supports what we see as an individual plant evokes the complexity of nature itself and our very limited understanding of it. The less-noticed wintergreen flowers resemble tiny, white, narrow-mouthed bells nodding singly from the leaf axils; the flower's calyx transforms into the better known cherry-red, berry-like fruit.

Wintergreen is eaten by virtually everything, including small birds, grouse (it is also known as "partridge berry"), ducks, squirrels, deer, bears, and people. The berry's spicy mint flavour is as refreshing as the Canadian north woods themselves. I continually snack on them while hiking, they're quite firm so they don't smash in my pockets, and they can be used in pies. The aromatic smaller leaves (known as "youngsters") are often chewed directly, and leaves of any age can be brewed into tea (wintergreen is also known as "teaberry") or refined into the well-known oil of wintergreen. This distinctive flavour is replicated in everything from candy to chewing gum.

As I contemplate a tiny wintergreen plant at the edge of November snow near Loon Lake, I am reminded of William Blake's renowned lines from "Auguries of Innocence":

> To see a World in a Grain of Sand
> And a Heaven in a Wild Flower
> ...
> Keeps the Human Soul from Care.[1]

Blake's observation stands the test not only of the human imagination, but of modern conservation biology as well, because there is a heaven to be seen in this wildflower. It is rooted with moss in a bit of shallow glacial till for soil, also supporting a mature stand of white pines on a granite outcrop jutting into Loon Lake, in the mixed hardwood of the Great Lakes–St. Lawrence forest region, underlain by the parent material of the Canadian Shield, in the eastern part of the North American continent, at 45° 45' latitude and 70° 45' longtitude in the Western Hemisphere of planet Earth, in the solar system orbiting a star we call the Sun, which is moving through the Orion spiral arm of the several-hundred-billion-star Milky Way galaxy, which is part of the Local Group of galaxies, knotted together into a larger supercluster of at least five thousand galaxies, of which at least fifty billion are currently thought to make up the Universe. The beautiful, small wintergreen (itself made up of tissues, cells, molecules, atoms, protons, neutrons, quarks, electrons, neutrinos, and leptons) can exist only because it is nested in, and nourished by, an expanding series of interacting ecological envelopes which quite literally give it life.

In 1981, when we founded the Canadian Council on Ecological Areas, ecologist Stan Rowe quipped that we should really have called it the Canadian Council on Ecological *Volumes*. This, he argued, would encourage humans to think of ecosystems three-dimensionally or volumetrically, and as being nested within each other like Russian dolls. Blake, therefore, could just as well have observed that we can "See a wild flower in a Heaven," but to do this we would have to begin from a different vantage point—with the largest Russian doll (the Universe) and think inward. Again, each ecological envelope forms the context and is a precondition for the next, peeling each back until we reach the tiny inner doll (the wildflower).

The image conjured up resembles nested segments of a magnificent "telescope of being," whose full expansiveness can be appreciated by peering in from either end, smaller to larger or larger to smaller, depending on where the viewer is located. By design or by chance, we humans were located somewhere toward the small end of the great telescope of being, here on Earth. It is therefore from *this* place that we can glimpse and marvel at things larger and smaller that form the life-giving context for wintergreen and people alike.

At the age of seven I first experienced Canada from the air, flying Trans Canada Airlines (in an old prop-driven North Star) from Ontario to visit my grandparents' farm in Saskatchewan. I remember staring fascinated, nonstop, out the window at the natural quilt of my country—the lakes, rivers, forests, and fields. At night, only the occasional twinkling light portrayed the lives of Canadians embedded in the landscape below. Later, in 1958, I "ground-truthed" much the same journey by bus, out of the north woods, across the prairies, and into the foothills to Banff when that town was still a rustic little mountain community. These were deeply formative experiences for me.

Today my work takes me back and forth across Canada perhaps twenty times a year. Still, my eye is held captive by the beauty gliding by that airplane window. Still, when I'm returning over the Atlantic my heart bumps when the first glimpse of home is the wild coast of Labrador—such a contrast to the entirely civilized land I last touched in Europe. And I can only imagine the likes of astronaut Roberta Bondar, "coming home to Canada" again and again as she orbited the earth. That experience also left her firmly committed to conserving the bits of wild fabric we still have in this part of the world. As Canadians and all citizens of the world move into the first century of a new millennium, we must decide what role we want wilderness to play in our lives and what provision we are prepared to make for it. We are likely the last generation to have any choice in the matter.

Ironically, it is technology, which we have traditionally used to devastate so much of the earth, that may now help us to save it. Technology linked with wisdom, that is. Through humans travelling by airplane or spacecraft, or through technological extensions of humanity such as the Hubble telescope, we have a profound opportunity to situate ourselves. When afforded that opportunity, we have indeed marvelled at what we saw, when looking further out, for example, to see stars or galaxies in virtually every direction, as in the now famous "Hubble Deep Field" poster, or when looking back on our own blue home planet. At moments like this, we are reminded that "ecology" is derived from the Greek word *oikos*, which means "home."

When a humble wintergreen plant, my modest cabin on Loon Lake, our species, and our Earth are perceived and understood in this broader context, it gives deeper meaning to the nature of life itself—a wonderful gift from all that permeates and surrounds. In his collection of essays on ecology called *Home Place*, Rowe shows us that life is a property vested not in individual organisms, but in the "global environment (the ecosphere) from which all evolved and by which all are sustained" (1990, 117).

It follows that, to save life on Earth, we must save the very preconditions for life. Therefore, saving species means saving places, means saving the life-giving ecological processes that make species and places possible. And the processes that sustain us can be understood as extending well beyond our earthly ecosphere to the realms that make our ecosphere possible, namely, the star nurseries wherein planets, suns, and galaxies themselves are still being born.

For now, there's not much we can do to conserve star nurseries. But the Earth's ecosphere is another matter. Step one is realizing that this is what we are truly trying to save.

To aid my own understanding of what's at stake, I find another image helpful, borrowed from Newfoundland and Labrador wildlife biologist Dennis Minty. Think of our planet as an apple. In cross-section, the apple has a large inner white part and a thin outer skin. These are analogous to the earth's abiotic core and the thin sensitive ecosphere wherein exists all life as we know it. The ecosphere is in fact a phase boundary, the point of interface between land, oceans, and air. You and I are positioned and existing right now in this phase boundary. We could not exist without it. Along with all other living things, we reside here in the skin of the apple, here in a vital, breathing membrane—a blue-green film of life energized by the sun.

Earth's continents, oceans, and biomes, such as forests, deserts, mountains, and grasslands, are like curved jigsaw pieces that fit together to form the round enveloping ecosphere. So words like "mosaic" and "quilt," just like the image of seeing a heaven in a wildflower, are more than compelling poetry. They are also very good biology. And the species that tend to interest naturalists so much—fascinating creations like birds, animals, and wintergreen flowers—are almost imperceptible specks inhabiting these puzzle pieces that make up the apple's skin. The specks are entirely the products of, and nourished by, the living ecosphere. Conversely, if we lose or impair a critical number of the specks, we endanger the larger puzzle pieces, and by extension the entire ecosphere.

Like an apple's skin, some parts of the Earth's ecosphere have been severely bruised or scarred. The top and bottom of the Earth-apple's skin, for example, are experiencing serious tears through holes in the ozone layer. These tears may be causing dramatic declines in some of the specks world-wide, in species like reptiles and amphibians. And entire areas of the apple's skin-surface are being degraded by pollution, especially the oceans, or by deforestation or desertification, in the case of the land components.

The point is that it is not just the species-specks that we are now in danger of losing. We are jeopardizing the membrane itself—our life-support system. If we focus all our attention on the specks, rather than saving the life-conveying skin, we are in danger of fiddling while Rome burns. What's at stake is the crucible of life itself—the evolutionary potential of our planet. Understood in this way, the true scale of modern conservation becomes clear, which in turn helps us set meaningful benchmarks for success.

Now, do all of these metaphors—ecological envelopes, nesting Russ-ian dolls, the great telescope of being, and some ecospheric skin of the apple—really flood over me simply at the sight of a tiny wintergreen plant? Frankly, yes, because this is what *all* living things bring to mind. Obviously, something other than wintergreen could equally serve as the medium or "wildflower" through which we all can "see a Heaven," in Blake's words. And no doubt there are other metaphors or images that could help us to bet-ter understand the nature of nature. But a transformation of that under-standing is deeply needed if we are to avoid squandering the wildflowers heaven has given us.

In practical terms, of course, natural delights such as wildflowers and wintergreen are not anyone's possessions at all, even on private land. Because land ownership does not make these things "mine," so much as it allows me to influence what happens to them. And that influence can be exercised responsibly or not. Leopold's guidance on this matter was: "A thing is right when it tends to preserve the integrity, stability and beauty of the biotic community. It is wrong when it tends otherwise" (1949, 240).

These are the perspectives and core values that must drive a land ethic, not just for Loon Lake but for our country and our planet. Without such an ethic, all other human strivings will amount to little or nothing.

Note

1 William Blake, "Auguries of Innocence," in *Blake: Complete Writings*, ed. Geoffrey
   Keynes (London: Oxford University Press, 1972), 431.

Works Cited

Leopold, Aldo. *A Sand County Almanac and Sketches Here and There*. New York:
   Oxford University Press, 1949.

Medsger, Oliver Perry. *Edible Wild Plants*. New York: Macmillan, 1939.

Rowe, Stan. *Home Place: Essays on Ecology*. Edmonton: NeWest, 1990.

11

Listening to Our Ancestors

Rebuilding Indigenous Nations in the Face of Environmental Destruction

Leanne Simpson

I have worked on a variety of environmental issues affecting indigenous territories for the past six years. Initially, I naively believed that Western science and Indigenous Knowledge working together could find answers to some of the environmental problems facing Indigenous and non-Indigenous communities. I now recognize that environmental issues within Indigenous Territories are ultimately justice issues. The roots of environmental destruction on Indigenous lands can be traced to colonization, colonial policies, and the Canadian state's experiment with forced assimilation. Until these injustices and abuses of power are rectified, and Indigenous Peoples regain control over our territories and communities, Western science will continue to be the primary tool the dominant society uses to justify the destruction of the environment, and Indigenous Knowledge will continue to provide Indigenous Peoples with the foundation to resist.

Our Elders tell us that just as it has taken five hundred years to create the colonial relationship we struggle against today, it will take that long again to complete the decolonization of our minds and knowledge, to reclaim our cultures, and to reinstate our traditional systems of governance. These are necessary prerequisites for the restoration of our societies to healthy and sustainable Nations. The question is, what will be left of the land after another five hundred years of exploitation that supports unfettered economic and industrial growth?

Indigenous Nations currently face some of the most devastating effects of environmental destruction in Canada. The Gwitch'in and First Nations in the Yukon are battling toxic contamination brought to their territories through long-range transport, industry, and government ignorance. Inuit Elders in Nunavut warn of the dire consequences of global warming as they witness accelerated climate change. The Mohawks of Akwesasne in southeastern Ontario continue to fight against industrial contamination of their waters, air, land, fish, and animals. The Pimicikamak Cree Nation in northern Manitoba demand to be treated fairly and equitably by governments responsible for flooding 1.2 million hectares of their land for hydroelectric development. The Innu Nation in Labrador confront low-level military flight testing on their territory in addition to mining and forestry interests. Burnt Church First Nation in New Brunswick continue to exercise their Treaty Right to fish lobster despite non-Native violence and injustice on the part of the Department of Fisheries and Oceans. Métis farmers in Manitoba and Saskatchewan are concerned with the impact of biotechnology on their traditional seed stocks. In the West, the Haida Nation are working to protect their forests from unsustainable industrial clear-cutting, while the Nuu-chah-nulth try to protect their lands from the impacts of tourist development and deforestation, and their waters from exploitation.

These struggles are not easy. Indigenous Peoples often find themselves challenging government-supported multinational corporations who exploit their territories for profit with no acknowledgment that their operations are on Indigenous lands, or that the industrial waste products they produce have a negative impact on local Indigenous communities. At the same time, much of the intact wilderness Canadians enjoy is a direct result of Indigenous Peoples' knowledge and sustainable ways of life. Issues of environmental protection and the management of natural resources cannot be resolved until the colonial relationship Canada insists on having with Indigenous Peoples is dismantled, and jurisdiction over Indigenous lands is restored to the hands and hearts of Indigenous Peoples.

For me, dismantling the colonial relationship between Canada and Indigenous Nations requires a reconstruction of Canadian history. Usual renditions marginalize the impacts of colonization and colonial policies on Indigenous Nations, as well as their resistance to such forces. Contrary to the standard racist and stereotypical images of historical Indigenous Peoples, our Elders tells us that Indigenous Nations were strong, healthy societies with complex knowledge and value systems, structures of governance, healing and wellness philosophies, and sustainable ways of living. Taiaiake Alfred, Rotinoshoni (Mohawk) scholar writes: "At the time of their first contact with Europeans, the vast majority of Native American societies had achieved true civilization: they did not abuse the earth, they promoted communal responsibility, they practiced equality in gender relations, and they respected individual freedom" (22).

It is well documented by the early Europeans that the land, forests, fish, and animals were plentiful and in good health at the time of contact. This is a testament to the values, knowledge, and respectful way of life practised by the members of Indigenous Nations. Indigenous systems of governance, from the Longhouse tradition of the Haudenosaunee to the Clan Systems of the Anishinaabeg and Mi'kmaq, to the Hereditary Chief and Potlatch systems of the west coast, are diverse, but common in that the environment was integrated into all aspects of governance and all decision-making processes. Decisions were made on a long-term basis, carefully considering any potential impacts they might have on the children, women, men, Elders, plants, and animals—on the land and in the Spirit World.

In the time before contact, Indigenous Nations were healthy, sustainable societies. The colonial assault on Indigenous Governance, languages, Knowledge systems, spiritualities, world views, and ways of living was also an assault on the environment. As the European colonizers exploited the animals, fish, and trees for economic gain, they also implemented sophisticated policies aimed at eliminating Indigenous Nations. Maintaining domination over the land and Indigenous Peoples has characterized the relationship between settler governments, the environment, and Indigenous Nations. The effects of colonization, colonial domination, and environmental destruction on Indigenous Peoples and their Territories present them with some of the most catastrophic environmental problems in Canada today.

Colonization, Colonialism, and Environmental Destruction

The Innu detest what the governments have done to our land. There has been heavy destruction of our homeland. We have been gentle and loving to our land, and we use it wisely. With the Churchill Falls development, all the animals were wasted away with the flooding. They dammed Mista-paustuk from very far away when we walked through nutshimit (the country). The governments didn't look at the Innu way of life. They never even consulted us. All that mattered to them were dollar signs, the profits, the jobs and the power that would be generated. The power lines go for thousands of miles, to places like New York and Montreal. Millions of dollars are made from our land every day. It doesn't matter to government and industry how much they destroy Innu land. (Byrne and Fouillard 2000, 157–58)

This quote by Innu grandmother Elizabeth Penashue summarizes the feelings of many Indigenous Peoples with regard to the dominant society and the government's treatment of the land and Indigenous Peoples. Although Penashue is commenting on contemporary situations, her words are also useful in examining the link between the colonization of Indigenous Peoples and environmental destruction.

When the European governments began to assert their authority over Indigenous Nations and Indigenous lands, they did so primarily for economic reasons. The colonizers made treaties with Indigenous Nations in central Canada because they were interested in securing the land for future white settlement and gaining access to "natural resources" (Final Report of the Royal Commission on Indigenous Peoples, vol. 2, 1996). Indigenous Nations forged treaty relations with Europeans because they were interested in protecting their lands, preserving their way of life for future generations, and setting out the terms for peaceful coexistence on a Nation-to-Nation basis. To Indigenous Peoples, treaties were and remain sacred relationships between two parties and the Creator. They are everlasting.

As settler governments gained numeric superiority, they were able to ignore the spirit and intent of those treaties. By the end of the Treaty-making period, negotiations were often held under inequitable conditions, with Canadian negotiators backed by superior military power. Indigenous communities were often ravaged by disease and death imported from Europe, and by the beginning of the twentieth century many leaders felt that they had no choice but to sign these weak agreements—the alternative being that the Europeans would have gone ahead and done what they wanted with the people and the land, with or without an agreement.

It is also important to examine the intentions of the Canadian government at this time. The Indian Acts of the late 1800s and early 1900s were in place during the major treaty negotiating period in central Canada. These acts made traditional forms of government and leadership illegal. The Potlatch and Sun Dance ceremonies were outlawed, but Elders from across Canada report practising ceremonies deep in the bush or during the night to avoid harassment and persecution by Indian Agents and RCMP officers. People were not allowed to leave the reserve without permission from the Indian agent, and they were not allowed to hire legal counsel or organize politically, making it nearly impossible to mobilize. Women were not allowed to vote, which effectively removed them, in addition to children and the Elders, from the decision-making roles they held in traditional governments. People were not allowed to wear their traditional clothes in public, and children were required to attend state-run schools, which either removed families from the land as they moved to settlements so their children could attend or forced children into abusive residential schools. The Indian Act controlled virtually every aspect of life and many of the more restrictive of these measures were not lifted until the 1950s. These policies were designed to destroy Indigenous governments, undermine Indigenous Peoples' relationship to the land, and assimilate them into the white Christian mainstream of colonial society.

It is during this period that we start to see the impact of colonization on the forests, animals, and fish in Indigenous Territories. The fur trade decimated beaver populations in regions where commercial trapping was driven by the price of pelts. Forests in southeastern Ontario and Quebec were demolished to support European shipbuilding enterprises supporting war efforts. Fish stocks in the inland lakes of central Canada began to crash as unsustainable commercial fishing by the colonizers seriously depleted the stocks. The construction of the railway signified the end of the buffalo and the way of life of the buffalo Peoples.

Environmental destruction and denial of Indigenous sovereignty continues today. Despite the hostile conditions, our Ancestors were strong and courageous. Many of them resisted colonialism and assimilation and worked to protect their languages, spiritualities, knowledge systems, way of life, and the land. It is a testament to them that we are still here today, able to share our knowledge with those who will listen and use it in good ways. It is our Ancestors who worked so hard to ensure that Indigenous values and philosophies were passed down to their children and their grandchildren's grandchildren. The reclamation of Indigenous lands, the revitalization of Indigenous traditions of governance and cultural teachings, and the revival of Indigenous environmental philosophies are the direct result of the strength of our Ancestors and the determination and commitment of Indigenous Peoples in Canada.

Indigenous Environmental Philosophies

Despite centuries of injustice, Indigenous Peoples have continued to pass their knowledge and values down to younger generations. Many non-Indigenous people are becoming interested in Indigenous environmental perspectives as their own cultures face global environmental crises. This outside interest in the philosophies of Indigenous Peoples has created both an opportunity for sharing and understanding and the potential again to exploit Indigenous Peoples and appropriate their Knowledge.

Indigenous Knowledge and cultures are diverse and unique. There are, however, some common themes and principles that emerge when it comes to describing Indigenous philosophies about land and life. In essence, these philosophies are complex and intricate. It is impossible to gain a full understanding of their meanings by simply reading about them. To gain a true understanding requires one to be taught for decades by accomplished Elders using traditional ways of teaching and transmitting knowledge. What I present here is a glimpse of some of the philosophies Indigenous Peoples have regarding the land and our relationship to it.

Indigenous world views or philosophical traditions view humans not only as part of the environment or the complex web of life, but as the environment itself. The environment is not only the outer space that people interact with, it is also a space inside of each living being and a place in the spirit world. Thus, words such as nature and environment, which in the English language denote the natural world but not necessarily humans, seem inappropriate or lacking when attempting to describe Indigenous understandings and constructions of the world. Sakej Youngblood Henderson, a Chickasaw scholar, explains:

> Most Indigenous peoples, for example the Mikmaq on the Atlantic coast, have no sound for nature. The best translation of their natural context is "space" or "place of creation" (*kisu'lt melkiko'tin*). They call their understanding of the sea, rivers, and forests where they live the realm of the earth lodge (*maqmike-wi'kam*).... The earth lodge is understood as an interrelated space where Indigenous people have direct and extremely visceral relationships with the essential forces in nature. (2000, 257)

If humans are in essence the environment, then when the environment is sick, humans will also be sick. This comes from an interconnection and interdependence that Indigenous Peoples have to and on the land, waters, air, sun, moon, animals, plants, and spirits. Cree grandmother Margaret Sam-Cromarty explains:

> Understand the wisdom of our people. They belonged to the earth. They believed that the earth was something to care for and not simply something to be subdued or ravaged for its wealth. How would you feel seeing a member of your own family brutalized repeatedly for another's gain? The earth is our mother. Our connection to the land is as to a beloved person. It is our land, our earth, and we love it. Now it is wounded by hydroelectric dams, and behind them by great man-made lakes. (1997, 104)

Within Indigenous environmental philosophies, there is an acknowledgment that all of life is related and that all of our actions and choices have impacts on other living beings. Decision making takes these impacts into account and humans are expected to act responsibly. Balance, respect, and responsibility characterize this philosophy:

> That place is one of balance and respect. The Creator, Sonkwaiatison, gave a gift to our people: awareness that our existence as human beings is embedded in a web of life that encompasses the entire universe. But this knowledge brings with it responsibility, and in that, we have a profound responsibility to ensure that we demonstrate respect and promote balance and harmony in all of our relationships. We are responsible for ensuring that the Creator's balance is maintained. (Alfred n.d., 8)

According to the Haudenosaunee teachings, humans are not the only beings with responsibilities. Plants, trees, water, and animals all have specific roles and responsibilities. The Kʷakʷaka'wakʷ people of Vancouver Island acknowledge the plants, trees, salmon, and animals for giving up their lives so that the people can live (Sewid-Smith [Kʷakʷaka'wakʷ] and Dick [Kʷakʷaka'wakʷ] 1998). For the Okanangan Nation, every part of daily life, including gathering food and making clothes, was a spiritual act (Armstrong [Okanagan] 1996). To Indigenous Peoples, the Spirit World is as real and powerful as the physical. Spirituality provides the foundation for Indigenous Knowledge systems and philosophies regarding humans and the environment:

> To the Gitksan and Wet'suwet'en, human beings are part of an interacting continuum which includes animals and spirits. Animals and fish are viewed as members of societies which have intelligence and power,

and can influence the course of events in terms of their interrelation-
ship with human beings.... To the Gitksan and Wet'suwet'en, time is
not linear but cyclical. The events of the "past" are not simply history,
but are something that directly effects the present and the future.
(1992, 23)

For the Anishinaabeg people, humans are not only part of an interacting
continuum, but they are the least powerful and most dependent beings in
the continuum. Humans are dependent upon the plants, animals, and spirits for their survival. As such, humans must exercise great humility and
respect for all elements of Creation. From the Anishinaabeg perspective,
humans do not have the right or the knowledge to control or manage other
beings.

It is these teachings and philosophies that provide Indigenous Peoples
with the strength to continue in their role as caretakers of the natural environment. Indigenous communities often find themselves on the front line,
living daily with the consequences of industrial contamination, large-scale
corporate development, and massive deforestation. The following section
explores some of the environmental issues Indigenous communities face in
Canada.

The Impact of Environmental Issues on Indigenous Peoples

Industrial Contamination

First Nation and Métis communities in the boreal regions of Canada are
working hard to protect their traditional territories from industrial deforestation as greedy multinational forestry companies move north in their
search for trees. Grassy Narrows First Nation, an Anishinaabeg community
in northwestern Ontario, are not only resisting massive deforestation
throughout their hunting and trapping grounds but are also recovering from
intense mercury contamination of the Wabigoon River in the 1960s, and
the relocation of the community to allow for expanded hydroelectric development one year later (LaDuke 1999). It was not long after this relocation
that the elders and community members began to notice damage to the
river and the fish, and since the Anishinaabeg were fishing in the Wabigoon
River, the contamination eventually reached the people. In 1975, the Ontario
government finally admitted that 20 to 30 percent of the residents showed
symptoms of mercury poisoning (LaDuke 1999). This resulted in the clo-
sure of the commercial and food fishery and the destruction of the traditional

economy. Despite all of this injustice, the people of Grassy Narrows remain strong and continue to put pressure on governments to stop the destruction of their territory and to take the health concerns of the Anishinaabeg people seriously.

Similar stories can be found in southern Ontario and in the far north. Dene and Inuit peoples are concerned about toxic contaminants, such as DDT and PCBs, left in their territories by the US government during the construction of the Alaskan Highway and the operation of Distant Early Warning (DEW) stations during the Cold War. More contaminants reach the fragile Arctic environment through long-range atmospheric transport. In the south, the Mohawks of Akwesasne are also battling to protect their traditional foods, waters, and people from corporate contamination, including PCBs from General Motors' dumping of contaminated materials, resulting in the widespread contamination of local groundwater (LaDuke 1999). Mohawk women have been the leaders in this fight, and are particularly concerned about toxic industrial chemicals present in their breast milk.

> Mohawk mothers voiced their anger at the contamination and the impact on their way of life. "Our traditional lifestyle has been completely disrupted, and we have been forced to protect our future generations. We feel anger at not being able to eat the fish. Although we are relieved that our responsible choices at the present protect our babies, this does not preclude the corporate responsibility of General Motors and other local industries to clean up the site." (Katsi Cook, in LaDuke 1999, 20)

Many of the people in these territories continue to rely upon traditional food sources for sustenance and good health and well-being. Even in the south, Indigenous Peoples continue to consume more fish, wild meat, wild rice, plants, and berries than the non-Native population. Our Elders tell us that eating our traditional foods will provide us with good health in the future (McDonald, Arragutainaq, and Novalinga 1997). Yet Indigenous Peoples are concerned that the plants, animals, and fish are becoming sick. Elders have witnessed changes in the quality and health of the animals and fish. Traditional foods provide Indigenous Peoples with much more than just calories.

The Power-Hungry South

Non-Indigenous Peoples in the southern parts of Canada rarely think twice about turning on lights, TVs, and appliances, nor do they know where their electricity comes from. The energy required to run a consumer-driven society is often provided by large-scale hydroelectric dams, built on Indigenous lands, usually without their consent and with little thought for the devastating impact the development has on the land, people, fish, plants, and animals. Sadly, it is difficult to find a Métis or First Nations community in northern Quebec, Manitoba, or Ontario that has not felt the destructive impact of hydroelectric development in their traditional territory. Many Anishinaabeg and Cree Elders remember not being told that dams were going to be built until construction was well underway. Only then did governments make meagre attempts at compensating Anishinaabeg and Cree communities for the flooding of their territories; destroying sacred sites and burial grounds, fish habitat, and spawning grounds; disrupting moose habitat and caribou migration patterns; disrupting and sometimes reversing the flow of lakes and rivers, thereby destroying traditional travel routes (Hertlein 1999). The dams also came with large contaminant ponds that polluted the waters, sediments, fish, and birds with methyl mercury. Road building increased access to territories thereby increasing industrial development (Ransom). Communities also face constantly fluctuating water levels, making river and lake travel unsafe and producing dangerous ice conditions in the winter, in addition to decimating fish-spawning areas.

Northern Canada provides electricity to southern regions, but provinces also export large quantities of power to the northern United States. Indigenous Peoples see none of the revenue generated from such exports but live each day with the impact of hydroelectric development. Hydroelectric power is far from the clean energy source touted by governments, and Indigenous Peoples have taken this message to international audiences as a way of putting pressure on provincial governments. Two Cree nations in Canada have launched consumer-awareness campaigns in the United States, drawing national and international attention to the environmental and cultural impacts of hydroelectric development. Cree activism and campaigning in Canada, the United States, and Europe, along with a highly critical report on Hydro Quebec's environmental impact statement by the review body conducting the environmental and social impact assessment on the Great Whale River Project, eventually led the Quebec government to abandon the proposed development. Similarly, the Pimicikamak (Cross Lake) Cree Nation of northern Manitoba have resisted accepting a large cash settlement from Manitoba Hydro, instead lobbying to have the terms of the Northern Flood Agreement honoured, a treaty signed by the Cree, Manitoba Hydro, the province of Manitoba, and the federal government. The Northern Flood

Agreement included a cash settlement for destroyed lands and several clauses relating to community development and remediation for damaged lands. However, the provincial and federal governments have not lived up to the terms of the agreement. The leaders of Pimicikamak First Nation say that more than one million hectares of land have been affected by Manitoba Hydro, leaving the community to deal with fish contaminated with methyl mercury, constantly changing water levels, destruction of moose habitat, changes in caribou migratory patterns, destruction of Cree travel ways, unsafe ice conditions in the winter, destruction of spawning areas, destruction of traditional recreation areas, and the degradation of the traditional economy (Hertlein 1999).

Corporate Deforestation

> When I connected to the Earth, it was like a mirror, like seeing myself. And when I saw a crane or a bulldozer digging into the Earth, it was like a form of rape. I just felt like that machine was scarring me. I began to realize that Earth is Woman and what happens to woman happens also to her. And she's feeling that. (Edna Manitowabi, quoted in Anderson 2000, 183)

Indigenous territories in the boreal regions contain some of the most lucrative forest in Canada. Deforestation is occurring in these regions at an alarming rate and communities have virtually no means of protecting their territories from corporate logging interests. The impact of deforestation on local communities is great: animal habitats are destroyed; sacred areas are ruined; traplines are rendered unproductive for decades; road building increases access to the land and cross-cuts animal migration routes; traditional plants and medicines are destroyed; and forests are replaced by monoculture tree farms, complete with pesticides and insecticides. Traditional economies are destroyed, and governments and industry justify their actions by producing a few jobs while raking in large profits. The majority of Indigenous People in these communities continue to live in economic poverty with the knowledge that their traditional homelands are being destroyed. As in other regions of Canada, however, Indigenous Peoples in the boreal forests are not just sitting by and allowing this to happen. They have built alliances with environmental and social justice groups, actively protested, launched consumer boycott and education campaigns, and exercised their jurisdiction over their lands.

Another Wave of Colonialism: Globalization and Free Trade

Indigenous Peoples worldwide have mobilized and joined the massive protests against the World Trade Organization (WTO) and the proposed Free Trade Area of the Americas (FTAA). Our experiences with five hundred years of colonization tell us that all Canadians need to turn their attention to the closed-door negotiations that will have tremendous implications for the environment and the lives of Indigenous Peoples.

Turning away from local economies toward global markets and economies means turning away from sustainable communities. The creation of consumer cultures at the expense of local indigenous ones; the emphasis on export rather than producing goods and services for the community; increased transportation and corporate competition, in addition to the elimination of national regulations to protect the environment—will all be devastating not only for the environment but for the very cultures that depend upon land, water, plants, and animals for their continued survival (Goldsmith 1996). Not only do these trade agreements threaten environmental protection, they also undermine Indigenous Knowledge and are in direct violation of Indigenous rights, both nationally and internationally (Manuel 2001).

Our traditional teachings tell us that we must treat our earth with respect and humility, and that we must change our unsustainable ways to ones based on traditional values. They warn that the consequences of greed, exploitation of natural resources, and consumerism will not make us healthy or well. If we listen to their teachings, then we should be terrified by the expanded economic growth and global development promised by trade agreements driven solely by corporate interests.

Conclusion

The legacy of colonization and colonial policies created a procession of injustices on the backs of Indigenous Peoples and the environment. Indigenous Peoples in Canada are working hard to reclaim their culture and knowledge, to reconnect to the land, to resist the continuous onslaught of colonialism, to rebuild our nations and traditions of governance, and to protect our Traditional Territories from environmental destruction. Supporting Indigenous Peoples in these endeavours is both a step toward the establishment of strong and sustainable Indigenous communities and the protection of the environment for future generations of Indigenous and non-Indigenous Peoples.

Works Cited

Alfred, Taiaiake (Mohawk). "The People." In *Words That Come before All Else: Environmental Philosophies of the Haudenosaunee*. Akwesasne, ON: Native North American Travelling College and the Haudenosaunee Environmental Task Force, n.d.

———. *Peace, Power and Righteousness: An Indigenous Manifesto*. Toronto: Oxford University Press, 1999.

Anderson, Kim (Cree/Métis). *A Recognition of Being: Reconstructing Native Womanhood*. Toronto: Second Story, 2000.

Armstrong, Jeanette (Okanagan). "Keepers of the Earth." In *Ecopsychology: Restoring the Earth, Healing the Mind*, ed. Theodore Roszak, Mary E. Gomes, and Allen D. Kanner. San Francisco: Sierra Club, 1996.

Final Report of the Royal Commission on Indigenous Peoples. Vol. 2. Ottawa: Minister of Supply and Services, 1996.

Gisday Wa (Wet'suwet'en) and Delgam Uukw (Gitksan). *Statements of the Gitksan and Wet'suwet'en Hereditary Chiefs in the Supreme Court of British Columbia 1987–1990*. Gabriola Island, BC: Gabriola Press, 1992.

Goldsmith, Edward. "Global Trade and the Environment." In *The Case against the Global Economy and for a Turn toward the Local*, ed. Jerry Mander and Edward Goldsmith. San Francisco: Sierra Club, 1996.

Hertlein, Luke (Cree). "Dams, Indigenous Peoples and Ethnic Minorities." In *Indigenous Affairs (International Work Group for Indigenous Affairs)* 3–4 (December 1999).

LaDuke, Winona (Anishinaabe). *All Our Relations: Native Struggles for Land and Life*. Boston, MA: South End, 1999.

Manuel, Art (Secwepemc). *The Free Trade of the Americas Agreement and the Threat to Indigenous Peoples*. Kamloops, BC: Interior Alliance Brief, 2001.

McDonald, Miriam, Luke Arragutainaq, and Zack Novalinga. *Voices from the Bay: Traditional Ecological Knowledge of the Inuit and Cree in the Hudson Bay Bioregion*. Ottawa: Canadian Arctic Resources Committee and Environmental Committee of Municipality of Sanikiluaq, 1997.

Penashue, Elizabeth (Innu). "Like the Gates of Heaven." In *It's Like the Legend: Innu Women's Voices*, ed. Nympha Byrne and Camille Fouillard. Charlottetown: Gynergy, 2000.

Ransom, Jim (Mohawk). "The Waters." In *Words That Come before All Else: Environmental Philosophies of the Haudenosaunee*. Akwesasne, ON: Native North American Travelling College and the Haudenosaunee Environmental Task Force, n.d.

Sam-Cromarty, Margaret (Cree). "Family Closeness: Will James Bay Be Only a Memory for My Grandchildren?" In *Defending Mother Earth: Native Amer-*

ican Perspectives on Environmental Justice, ed. Jace Weaver (Cherokee). New York: Orbis, 1997.

Sewid-Smith, Daisy (Kʷakʷaka'wakʷ), and Adam Dick (Kʷakʷaka'wakʷ). "The Sacred Cedar Tree of the Kwakwaka'wakw People." In *Stars Above, Earth Below: American Indians and Nature*, ed. M.C. Bol. Niwot, CO: Roberts Rinehard, 1998.

Youngblood-Henderson, James Sakej (Chickasaw). "Ayukpachi: Empowering Indigenous Thought." In *Reclaiming Indigenous Voice and Vision*, ed. Marie Battiste (Mi'kmaq). Vancouver, BC: University of British Columbia Press, 2000.

12

Cutting a Deal with Attila

Confrontation, Capitulation, and Resolution in Environmental Conflict

Ehor Boyanowsky

We need the tonic of wilderness, to wade sometimes
in marshes where the bittern and the meadow hen lurk and
hear the booming of the snipe; to smell the whispering sedge
where only some wilder and more solitary fowl builds her
nest....We can never have enough of nature. We must be
refreshed by the sight of inexhaustible vigor, vast and
titanic features....We need to witness our own
limits transgressed and some life pasturing
freely where we never wander.
—*Henry David Thoreau*

I can't remember when I first became fascinated by water. But by the time I was in high school, our team's bus crossing a bridge would trigger a mocking chorus of, "I wonder if there are any fish in that river?" from my teammates and the cheerleaders. Many times before they'd heard me wonder that out loud in so many words whenever we'd come upon a stream. On the trips to Dryden, a paper mill town of gray demeanour and sickly scented air ("the smell of money," retorted the locals to any complaint), we would often admire the rapids of the Wabigoon River, unaware that the foam had become a toxic brew of dioxins—mill effluent that, according to Lloyd Tataryn in his book *Dying for a Living*, merely for eating the fish they caught eventually condemned the aboriginal people of the White Dog Reserve to the neurological ravages of Minamata disease.

It was my father who used to take me fishing at Bug River Bridge on mosquito-infested evenings, with a bunch of men and women sitting on a riverbank watching their bobbers and drowning minnows. There was nothing to do. I was soon bored, hungry, covered in bites, and I wanted to go home. Besides, we almost never caught anything. Then one day some union organizers who came to town and stayed at our house wanted to go fishing. My father couldn't go so they took me. We fished in a rowboat parked under the Chukuni River Bridge and the fish, dozens of pickerel (walleyes), were biting. We came home with our limits. And I was hooked. Soon I was saving for a fishing rod and reel and after that, whenever I saved up thirty-nine cents, I bought a "Dardevil" spoon, and rode my bike or hitchhiked to the Forestry Bridge, where I often lost my lure on the third cast and went home dreaming of the time when I would have a whole tackle box full.

It was the beginning of a major reconnection with my dad, the passionate fisherman and now the maker of stainless steel spoons that I designed and then painted after he turned them out. When I started working for Ontario Central Airways as a teenager, we would fly out into the hinterland, and it was then that I realized I lived in a land that had a lake or pond within virtually every single mile, a dry, ten-mile, wooded stretch of forest in any direction being an oddity. I remember experiencing as a palpable thrill the realization that the millions of fish in those lakes, and the animals in the bush surrounding them, lived not because of man but in spite of him. It became a sign that all was well in that part of the earth. When I can find it, it still is.

More recently, I have come to understand that a person has to experience a thing of value before she or he can become concerned about its loss, and perhaps that is why people in Vancouver, even business people, are passionate about the environment and the threats to it, while people in Toronto, my birthplace, are not. You can live your whole life in Toronto without ever confronting any true wildness in nature. So in Toronto one thinks, "What's the big deal?" while in Vancouver I watch eagles wheeling in the sky as I write, and just last spring my English Setter pup went from carefree somnolence under my desk to berserk as I looked up to see a shimmering bear walk through my garden. Not that rural people, especially those living as wage slaves in Red Lake, Dryden, or Fort St. John, are paladins of the wilderness. If you are merely surviving in a one-industry town, first, last, and always, you want to feed your family, and if you are functioning on a higher economic plane, the next priorities in North America are a house and a vehicle. If those goals are threatened by job loss, all bets are off. My father's labour history taught me that. Instead, people have to equate their own survival with that of wildlife, wilderness, and the environment in general. And they must do it before it is too late to do the right thing.

It takes a while to figure things out. A child likes its father to be good and kind but also strong and unambiguous. In our town, the kind of place you fought your way into and out of, my friends' fathers weren't always saints, but they were definitive and strong. When you asked a question, for better or worse, you got a straight answer. And you were judged on how you behaved in public. Alas, my dad didn't fit into that mould. Once, when walking with a buddy and my dad, I came across an aboriginal man lying in a mud puddle. I exclaimed derisively, hoping to amuse my companions, "Look at that drunken Indian!" To my six-year-old surprise, my father said, "Son, don't judge a man on where he is until you know his history, how he got there." I remember my cheeks burning with shame at my father's lack of manly condemnation. Now I wish I had thanked him for it. Since that lesson I try for as long as possible to reserve my judgment, even of the logger who clear-cuts a forest or the capitalist who finances a mine polluting a major salmon stream or the gillnetter who wipes out rarer, more valuable fish, such as steelhead, in his frenzy to take for profit as many sockeye salmon as possible.

While at graduate school in the late 1960s, I was introduced to fly fishing by a fellow student from Massachusetts. Small streams—Black Earth Creek, Mount Vernon Creek—only miles from Madison, Wisconsin, became my sanctuary, the only places I could go without feeling I should be studying. It was the birth of the age of environmental awareness. For the first time, development, growth, and progress were being challenged by the mainstream. In the intimacy of those creeks I learned the relationship between the fish and me, but like all hunters and gatherers, I came to understand other things as well: how the fish lies where it does in order to acquire the most food with the least effort during those times when it is safest to do so; or if the hatch of insects becomes sufficiently great, how, in the safety of numbers, it tosses caution to the wind in favour of gorging itself on masses of protein.

It took me a whole year to start catching fish, for not only did I have to master the skill of casting a fly, a weightless lure, without creating a ruckus and spooking my quarry, but I also had to learn the currents of the river and what kinds of obstructions, stones, and other matter create the habitat fish need; how to present a fly in a natural drift that would not betray the presence of a line; what fly should be presented at what time; what water clarity, speed, temperature, chemistry, and depth promote the cycle of plants, then insects, and fish; and how even the presence of predators, I among them, creates a balance of life. In learning to cast you become a participant, but with the other knowledge you become, in a minor, local sense, an entomologist, a hydrologist, an ichthyologist, a botanist, eventually a deadly predator, and, as you realize the interdependence of all life forms in the ecology of the stream, a conservationist and environmentalist. When you reach that plateau—the consciousness of symbiosis—early in your development as a hunter and gatherer, it becomes self-evident that in order to survive you have to protect the creeks, rivers, and streams of the earth as you would the veins and arteries of your body. So you become incredulous, then enraged, that people are willing to destroy those vital flowing bodies of water, to channel them into flumes, to bury them in culverts and sewers.

Nova Scotia is, by North American standards, a very ancient place and, because recent development has passed it by, in relative terms, replete with wilderness. Living there in the early 1970s initially filled me with joy. But accompanying the thrill of exploring Atlantic salmon rivers open to all for angling was the realization that those rivers, naturally slightly acidic, had with the drift of deadly weather-borne acid rain from the industrial centres of the northeast United States become inhospitable to fish and were dying. Others were suffering from the effects of logging and farming that denuded banks and led to overheating and siltation of spawning beds. Then, overfishing by anglers, a new revelation some found hard to believe, came to light as well, compounding the effects of deadly gauntlets of gill nets in the estuaries and those of inshore boats. The final stroke was the discovery of the feeding grounds of migrating salmon under the icefields off Greenland and their wholesale slaughter by Danish and Faroe Islander boats.

The realization was sinking in that no place, regardless how remote, was safe from the ravages of civilization and a faceless technology that served the master of human greed without conscience. On the east coast, the first environmentalists were members of angling organizations who, because they were on the streams and engaged with their quarries rather than blithely hiking by as spectators, sounded the alarm. They were the first to discover the damage to streambeds, the empty spawning grounds, and the absence of insects and baby fish in water that was now clear and pristine, in the sense of becoming devoid of life. So long as there are predators, there are those who care desperately about their prey and will not settle for the survival of a token few. Angling organizations, such as the Atlantic Salmon Federation, led the battle against the despoilers.

Some members of the public argued, however, that anglers were merely self-interested killers who were selfish for trying to stop others from gainful employment in gillnetting, steel mills, logging, and farming. It became a standoff. Rather than concern for wildlife and wilderness being an intellectual process, it became increasingly clear that, at least in some measure, the sentiment and imagination of the public had to be captured. Just before his death, the poet Ted Hughes, whose background is English working class and not associated with fox hunting, an upper-class blood sport, pointed out the curious fact that research has revealed that fox populations were most buoyant when fox hunting was most popular and declined nearly to extinction when fox hunting was out of favour. That phenomenon can be explained, at least in part, because farmers who reap the rewards of fox hunting protect foxes when hunting is in vogue and otherwise try to exterminate them as pests. Perhaps what we are really promoting in opposition to fox hunting, rather than protection of the species, is "the unspeakable in full pursuit of the uneatable," as Oscar Wilde characterized the hunt.[1]

In 1970, at approximately the same time that a crisis was occurring on the waters of the east coast, environmentalism was being reincarnated on the west coast of Canada. There it was two-pronged. The three-member Don't Make a Wave Committee was angered by the Sierra Club, an old-time environmental organization based in California that refused to protest nuclear arms testing in Amchitka, Alaska. The many thousand member British Columbia Wildlife Federation, an organization of hunters and fishermen, formed a committee to address the precipitous decline in steelhead stocks. Steelhead, seagoing rainbow trout recently reclassified as salmon, are the rarest on the Pacific coast, the only species that doesn't die after spawning, and the one most revered by freshwater anglers. Greenpeace was spawned from the Don't Make a Wave Committee, and the Steelhead Society of British Columbia (SSBC) from the BC Wildlife Federation.

I arrived in Vancouver In 1974, and when the clouds finally lifted after a month, I began to recognize the extraordinary perch humankind had in this part of the world. Although the streams of Vancouver had been buried in culverts or reduced to storm sewers, on the north shore one could pass through the looking glass fifteen minutes from town and be on the Seymour River in almost total wilderness. The Seymour was spared from the developers' plans by its municipal watershed designation. Black bears fed on berries in my Deep Cove backyard and cougars prowled the rooftops. Killer whales patrolled Indian Arm and can still be seen from the home overlooking Howe Sound I moved to in 1988. An hour away, I occasionally encountered grizzly bears in the Squamish and Elaho River valleys that were, alas, quickly being strip-mined by logging.

I immediately joined Greenpeace and the BC Wildlife Federation, but then I went to an SSBC annual general meeting in a suburban community hall and was thrilled by what I saw—the whole spectrum, from backwoodsmen in Caterpillar tractor caps (before they became a fashion statement), to corduroy, denim, and flannel, to the dark suits of politicians and the tweed and serge of businessmen and academics. All were imbued with an unspoken common understanding and passion that I articulated only years later—that wild, unengineered rivers and wild steelhead, the symbol of Pacific salmon, are vitally important not only to those who pursue them for sport in order to reconnect the sacred hunter-prey relationship, even though those present were already releasing most of the fish they caught, but also as an index of how well the earth and ultimately the human race is doing.

Greenpeace, in its objection to nuclear testing, factory pollution, clearcut logging, seal and whale hunting, was grabbing most of the headlines and, I felt, doing good work. But looking back on the influences in my life, I realize now that closest to my heart were the intimate connection with rivers, fish, and scientifically based conservation positions, and educating the public to the importance of wild steelhead, among a wide diversity of members who read like a demography of British Columbia. In those days, slimy old fish, even the surpassingly beautiful steelhead, were not sexy; in fact, they were boring to the general public. We had our work cut out for us.

The preservation of rivers in their natural state faced opposition from many quarters. Logging interests wanted the giant trees that grew in the valley bottoms, right to the banks of the streams. Those trees were not only protecting the banks from erosion, but also providing a forest canopy for insects and birds and an arbour against overheating of small streams by the summer sun. Remarkably, there was no "green strip" of trees required by law to be left uncut, and even after the much-maligned (by industry) Forest Practices Code was enacted, I came across great streamside cedars felled right into the Nahmint River, an emerald jewel on the west coast of Vancouver Island. And once those trees were gone, the loggers moved higher into the mountains, logging on steep slopes that, even on non-fish-bearing tributaries, caused bank instability, erosion, and, ultimately, massive, rapid runoff.

The result was the transformation of meandering, slowly flowing creeks into straightened flumes carrying siltation that found its way down into the larger spawning tributaries, clogging the clean gravel and destabilizing the whole system. Now each new rainstorm exacerbated the situation. Even science colluded against conservation, for early inchoate research indicated that in streams denuded of trees on the bank, fry (baby salmon and steelhead who spend the longest time in freshwater) grew faster. That short-term effect was due to the warmer water of those suddenly exposed, previously icy streams. More recent results indicate that the streams deteriorate over time, become desiccated, and, as a result, spawning is vastly reduced, if not extinguished. Seasoned steelheaders knew that was the effect long before science caught up, but they faced opposition at public meetings.

A further problem, as stated earlier, was that the issue of logging pitted citizens of local communities, who saw any conservation measure as a threat to their jobs, against conservationists, who were characterized as outsiders or elitists. The situation became especially sensitive when a local chapter of the SSBC, for example, on Vancouver Island or the Queen Charlottes, comprised both loggers and other professions. At one meeting a local chamber of commerce type chastised me for demanding protection of a river, saying we would have to share and that the valley would be returned to us after it had been clear-cut. I responded that that would be like Attila the Hun riding into our town, announcing his intent to plunder and destroy, and our replying, "Well, will you settle for half?" Some things cannot be negotiated. Having recently visited Spain and Russia, where they have no giant, old growth trees but many historic monuments, I found that even those of czarist origin were lovingly preserved (and, after the devastation of the war, restored by the Communists). It brought home the realization that, although in British Columbia we do not have one-thousand-year-old, human-made monuments, we do have the trees. They belong to a world that is comforted to know they exist and, once they are gone, we will all be impoverished.

My campaigning for preservation of the very steep west side of the Squamish River, containing the last three untouched spawning tributaries (contrasted with the totally devastated east side where the main logging road runs), garnered me a spot on the blacklist when local loggers set up a roadblock in reaction to environmental protesters who opposed the logging of the Elaho Valley, a tributary of the Squamish, with its very ancient trees.

As the Squamish–Whistler area evolves from employment by mainly a single industry to a multi-faceted, recreational, and non-resource-extraction economy, more citizens see old growth trees from the perspective we have been propounding: namely, that those trees as the capital of our resource are irreplaceable and, as economist Harold Innis argued, should not be squandered.² In their stead we should be harvesting only second- and third-growth trees, and only when that harvest does no damage to the ecology of wildlife, wild fish, and wild rivers. Logging companies are recognizing the change in public values. In the past few years, two have actually received conservation awards from the Steelhead Society: West Fraser Timber, for giving up, without compensation, logging rights to the Kitlope Valley, the largest intact temperate rain forest watershed on the west coast; and Macmillan Bloedel, for giving up logging of old-growth forests and halting clear-cutting on steep slopes. In addition, Macmillan Bloedel has developed single-tree helicopter logging, undeniably in response to market pressures, such as the boycott of lumber from clear-cut, old-growth forests organized by Greenpeace. Although differences remain over logging the west side of the Squamish, the Habitat Restoration Corporation (HRC), a subsidiary of the Steelhead Society, has partnered with the logging company International Forest Products to restore vital spawning tributaries.

Another great threat to wild fish and rivers is dams, though many new dams are not likely to be proposed until the water-hungry, western United States makes a move to promote diversion of BC rivers south. The BC government ceded the water rights of a vast area west of Prince George to the Aluminum Company of Canada (Alcan) over fifty years ago to promote the building of a smelter at Kemano. The diversionary project took away over 50 percent of the flow from the Nechako River, a major tributary of the Fraser, the greatest remaining undammed salmon river on the west coast of North America.

It seems preposterous that, in the mid-twentieth century, the Carrier-Sekani aboriginal people returned from hunting to discover that the flooding had wiped out their traditional village and gravesites. They have been fighting for redress ever since. In the 1980s, Alcan announced it was going to exploit the rest of its water licence to build another smelter which would destroy several rivers, including the famed steelhead stream, the Bulkley River, and further reduce the Nechako to no more than 13 percent of its original flow. The Carrier-Sekani drew a line in the sand and were joined by a large coalition of residents and conservationists that rose in opposition to the project, though businesses and labour in Kitimat, the local company

town, supported it. In the fall of 1990, the Mulroney federal Conservative
government, and then the BC Social Credit and New Democratic governments, backed Alcan. The federal cabinet passed an Order in Council
exempting the company from a federal environmental review of what the
former Pacific coast director general of the DFO, Pat Chamut, called the
greatest environmental threat to west coast fisheries of the twentieth
century.

When many people asked me why I (along with many other members
of citizens' groups and the fishermen's union), representing the SSBC, continued to fight what was a fait accompli, I replied that some battles are
worth losing, and that I didn't want to have to explain to my children, when
the Fraser was eventually depleted and the Nechako moribund, how we
could have let such a thing happen. In my presentation at the eventual public hearing, I argued that the value of a river could not be assessed by com-
paring its fisheries and recreational income to the income that would derive
from hydroelectric power or another industrial use; instead, by using modern insurance underwriting criteria, we must consider the actual replacement
cost.

That is, we must assess the cost of creating such a riverine, ecosystem
with its variegated insects and varieties of fish that have adapted over many
centuries. We must factor in the aquatic plants and those that line the bank,
including trees, together with the birds and animals that coexist in that
environment. There are very few countries, much less corporations, that
could afford such an undertaking over the many years required to bring it
to fruition. In 1994, at the eleventh hour, the public suddenly took a vital
interest. Several very courageous Department of Fisheries and Oceans scientists blew the whistle on political skullduggery within the DFO, choos-
ing to go public and resign rather than go along with the handpicked, tame
replacement scientists who claimed that 87 percent of a river could be
diverted without harming the salmon runs. *Vancouver Sun* journalist Mark
Hume probed the story, revealing that a prominent University of British
Columbia scientist, formerly a fisheries champion, had taken a position on
Alcan's board of directors and was lobbying on its behalf.[3]

But finally the connection was made in the public mind that the so-
called Kemano Completion Project was not just a northern local issue. The
Fraser was going to be affected and its salmon runs, which had recently
been rendered almost extinct by a combination of bad management and
low, warm water, would be severely threatened. About that time, the president of the Bonneville Power Administration in Washington state revealed

that it was spending over $150 million US per year to alleviate the effects of that project on salmon, with very little success. The connection was made by the SSBC and others that the Fraser River was the main artery of British Columbia and as went the Fraser, so did the fortunes of the province.

Belatedly, the very popular talk show host Rafe Mair joined the fray and made it his mission to sway public sentiment against the project. To everyone's surprise, the opposition Liberal Party (usually pro-business) came out against Kemano Completion. The NDP government, having already made public its apologistic report by a University of Victoria professor who argued that most of the damage had been done in the original diversion, had no choice but to cancel the project and try to cut a deal with Alcan.

The half-built tunnel in the mountain was abandoned. Alcan held the high legal ground, but was perceived to be wallowing in the mire of environmental and social immorality along with the federal government and DFO, though its president argued that corporations are by definition amoral, having a fiduciary duty only to their shareholders. An environmental victory under impossible odds had been ostensibly won. The devil remained in the details, however, and in the ensuing years no final resolution of water problems lingering from the original project has been reached. The original coalition still toils on, now out of the public eye.

Another great issue affecting rivers, and even oceans—increasingly recognized, despite their vastness, as fragile and vulnerable—was pollution from pulp mills. In the late 1980s, technology revealed how incredibly lethal even a few parts per billion of dioxins and furans, by-products of the delignification process using chlorine, were to fish. Fin fish died very quickly and, more insidiously, the poisons accumulated in shellfish and other sedentary and residential species. The toxins quickly moved up the food chain to herons and raptors, such as eagles, and, eventually to people. In the winter of 1989, a coalition of environmental groups, once again including the SSBC and the Fishermen's and Allied Workers Union, was going to have a major press conference, revealing the amount of dioxins in paper milk cartons. Upon perusing recently released DFO studies, and having a background in research methods, I noticed that the amounts of toxic substances in shellfish harvested in Howe Sound were many times above the legal limit. The emphasis of the press conference was changed to focus on local shellfish. Public reaction was very strong and, perhaps purely by coincidence, Howe Sound was closed to shellfishing the next day.

Pop singer Terry Jacks, had, without success, been leading a renegade campaign against the pulp mill owners and the DFO for lack of enforcement of pollution laws, until European customers threatened a boycott of chlorine-bleached paper products. On December 13, 1990, the Social Credit Environment Minister John Reynolds resigned from cabinet when Premier Vander Zalm reneged on a bill for zero tolerance of pulp mill effluent. The bill was, however, finally effected soon after by the new NDP government. What was especially interesting in this case was that even pulp mill workers were blowing the whistle on the company, since their jobs were protected by union membership and their lives threatened by the common fate of dioxin poisoning. It became clear to affluent West Vancouver residents and pulp mill workers alike that a good income had no meaning if their environment, the fish in it, and eventually their children were to be exposed to deadly carcinogens. Fish were like the canaries in the coalmines—a harbinger of how well humans would do.

Because steelhead are the most primitive of the Pacific salmon, that is, the oldest, most direct descendant of the ancient polar salmon that split into Atlantic and Pacific families, they have colonized virtually every coastal watershed and even many of the far inland watersheds, with runs in the dozens to thousands entering a river every day of the year. Most rivers experience multiple runs of fish that appear in every season. They are the fewest in number of the anadromous *Oncorhynchus*, but the most resilient, not dying after spawning, and many making multiple returns to their natal rivers. All other anadromous Pacific salmon die after their spawning run, with the largest, the chinook, numbering in the tens of thousands, coho in the hundreds of thousands, and pinks, chums, and the most highly prized commercially, sockeye, under ideal conditions, running into the millions.

Originally, indigenous people took salmon using weirs, traps, and dip nets in the rivers, assuring that only those fish needed would be retained. When Europeans started to fish commercially, they regarded indigenous peoples as having an unfair advantage and, though the latter were extremely selective, their methods were banned and they were given gill nets and spears instead. In addition, commerical gill net fleets proliferated and, like so many thousands of medieval doomsday machines, wiped out any fish in their path. That was the fate even of those they did not target, especially steelhead and coho, which came to be worth their weight in gold to a burgeoning sport fishery on the ocean and in the rivers. Rather than managing for conservation of the rarest species, DFO officials defined their role as handmaidens of the powerful, commercial industry and chose to allow the decimation of steelhead stocks, as well as coho, mixed in with millions of sockeyes, chums, and pinks.

The most perverse example of such waste occurred on the Skeena River where, like so many other DFO projects, artificial spawning channels allowed the numbers of one strain of sockeye to skyrocket. This masked the actual fluctuating numbers of wild sockeye from many smaller systems and, with massive growth of the fishing fleet, resulted in extinction of many runs of sockeye and, even more tragically, steelhead and coho. The response of the commercial fishing lobby, including the fishermen's union, ironically, our ally on other issues, was to demand more hatcheries for artificial enhancement of all species, including steelhead, in order to compensate for the wild fish that were incidentally being wiped out.

Research, however, has supported the original contention of steelhead anglers that hatcheries are no replacement for wild fish. Wild fish have adapted to the peculiar characteristics of their watersheds over eons, and are much more robust and genetically honed to survive. Hatchery fish will, in the short term, reproduce well under pampered conditions but, unlike the product of genetic diversity and evolutionary adaptiveness, eventually become less and less robust and, as with monocultures on tree farms, increasingly vulnerable to disease. Dan Burns, president of the SSBC, characterizes hatcheries as "chemotherapy"—sometimes necessary for survival in extreme conditions but not the way to plan long-term good health; hence his creation of the Habitat Restoration Corporation in spring 1994 to ensure that natural spawning would replenish wild stocks, though over a much longer time span than hatcheries. In seven years, HRC projects have produced a half million wild adult salmon.

The Wild Steelhead Campaign of the SSBC highlighted the value of wild fish and brought the notion of wildness to the public using famed artists, films, and even poetry readings by Ted Hughes. With the threats to salmon from the foreign boats using fifty miles of driftnets to wipe out every species of fish, as well as millions of birds and mammals, and the salmon war between the United States and Canada raging, people suddenly started worrying about fish and relating them to the health of their rivers, their environments, and, on the east and west coasts, their own lives.

In 1993, at a Vancouver roundtable leading up to the United Nations Conference on the High Seas, very little of note was accomplished until the representatives of the commercial industry left the room. For the first time, I noted that a Greenpeace representative had made a presentation at a fisheries conservation meeting, promoting the "precautionary principle" of management. It was a clear sign that fisheries issues had gone mainstream, that fish, in addition to more visible, anthropomorphically friendly species

such as whales and seals, had become sexy. I was thrilled. I buttonholed
two of the participants whom I felt were among the more thoughtful individuals in the room, Dr. John Lien of Newfoundland and Chris Chavasse of
Alaska, and we drafted a resolution that, as a blueprint for fishing operations,
would go a long way toward reversing the destruction of the world's fisheries. The resolution included the following:

First: no fishing technique shall be allowed where a more selective
technique required to protect weak and/or threatened target or non-
target species exists. At present most fishing is done by gill nets that
entangle and kill all species indiscriminately, or by using seine nets—
bags that corral fish and are tightened and hauled over a drum at high
speed, killing or damaging all fish within. That could be avoided if the
seine was tightened gradually with the fish brailed (lifted out by dip
nets). The process would take much longer, but longer fishing times
would be allowed without threatening fish stocks. More people would
be employed, non-target fish returned unharmed, and monitoring would
be much easier. Such methods are ideal for shallow ocean-straddling
species.

Second: the exclusive use of estuarial traps and weirs for fish returning
to their natal streams (salmon, for instance) would eliminate inter-
ception by foreign vessels and give all the fish to the country of origin—
the one responsible for stewardship of spawning habitat. That principle
would eliminate the need for international commissions, salmon wars,
even costly boats, and allow strict monitoring and exact harvesting
targets.

Third: with ocean environment in such flux, those countries with the
greatest stewardship responsibility, given their vast coastlines—Canada,
Russia and the USA—must establish an alliance to regulate and police
their continental shelves for conservation of northern hemisphere,
deep-water species, regardless of arbitrary 200-mile limits.

In 1993 those suggestions were hooted at by the commercial interests.
By 1999, after more than one hundred years of wasteful, imprudent fishing
practices, many of them became de rigueur when David Anderson, a former
secretary of the South Vancouver Island Chapter of the SSBC, became federal minister of fisheries and, armed with scientific evidence that coho stocks
were at historic lows, implemented policies demanding almost no mortality of threatened wild coho. Anticipating those measures, I called a meetng
with the heads of the fishermen's unions and the vessel, gill net, and seine

boat owners on a Victoria Day weekend. They were astounded when I predicted Anderson would allow fishing only if there was zero mortality of wild coho. They thought a 20 percent tolerance would be allowed. When I assured them they were wrong, they wanted to know, given that we had "won the battle," why the SSBC was talking to them.

I pointed out that we did not want to eliminate the commercial fishery, we were only trying to shape its activities so that it did not destroy the common resource of wild fish, a resource many of them had advocated wiping out to allow gillnetters to operate unconstrained by concerns for other species. The DFO was suddenly reborn as a paladin of conservation, and most staff were thrilled. Many gillnetters went with the buyout offered, others adapted, and some even started experimenting with traps and beach seines. Traps, fish wheels in rivers, and brailing by seine netters became increasingly common. With luck, we were entering a new age of doing business.

The new way of business had to be entrenched because some were still just holding their breath, waiting for better times. Even worse, in order to settle land claims, rather than restricting future fishing to environmentally sound, selective fishing methods, the DFO was giving out gill net licences and special fishing opportunities to aboriginal groups that could come back to haunt the fishery and undo all the progress that had been made. In my opinion, the combination of privileged opportunity for one group, combined with the use of destructive, regressive methods, was a recipe for future conflict between aboriginal people and non-aboriginal Canadians, especially environmentalists. It was a totally unnecessary conflict, because many aboriginal groups were quick to embrace selective methods such as traps, weirs, and fish wheels—methods from their own cultural history—when given the opportunity.

Conclusion

Combining experience from my personal development, values, and background with concepts derived from my academic fields of social, environmental, and forensic psychology, I developed a theory that I hoped would delineate the events that occur when a populace is faced with environmental threat. An early version was presented at the World Congress of the International Society for Research in Aggression in 1990, and a later version was published in the volume *Water Export: Should Canada's Water Be for Sale?* in 1992. The theory proposes to predict the conditions under which, for example, environmental pollution or destruction would be tolerated by society, as opposed to when opposition would be mobilized that would result in civil disobedience or even terrorism. On the other hand, the theory allows for conditions under which a positive resolution could be reached.

There are three forces that affect action or change when a major social issue arises: public will, corporate will, and political will. Very often corporate and political will have a special arrangement allowing pollution or other environmental depredation, despite laws to the contrary, in order to provide jobs for the populace, benefits to the government, and, sometimes even to its individual members. As the environmental threat mounts and is recognized as a health hazard, especially if unemployment rises as job losses occur due to technological or corporate change, public concern in turn intensifies. Corporations with rising profits see new laws and even penalties as the cost of doing business. Community tolerance quickly declines as fear for the survival of a segment of the population rises. As a condition of common fate comes to be recognized, community opposition in the absence of government action and the resultant loss of government credibility mount until they culminate in civil disobedience and even acts of eco-terrorism (destruction of private property, even threats to lives).

In the case of dioxin pollution of Howe Sound, the grapevine had it that the government must enforce the Fisheries Act, which forbids the dumping of a substance deleterious to fish in a body of water they occupy. If it did not, sabotage, on the heels of protests against pulp mills, was imminent, given the mounting evidence of the contamination of shellfish and eventually fin fish, and the high incidence of lung cancer among non-smoking, downwind residents. The mills had permits allowing dumping, but studies had shown most mills in BC were out of compliance, and those in Howe Sound were among the worst. At the last moment, the government brought in a special bill forcing mills, at great cost, to eliminate dioxins from their effluent.

In the case of Kemano Completion, the government had capitulated to the corporation in the original agreement, creating terrible health threats to the Carrier Sekani through mercury contamination of the fish in the lake produced by the flooding and the destruction of their hunting lands. But it had also created jobs and wealth and that set up a standoff. However, when the public learned that the second phase of the project had been exempted from the government's own laws (that is, by a federal environmental review), and that the health threat was going to approach common fate proportions by endangering the Fraser, direct action was mobilized. Again at the eleventh hour, the government acted, public and political wills were joined, and civil disobedience was avoided.[4]

Both of these environmental conflicts have been analyzed from an anthropocentric perspective based on values affecting people's welfare. Where, however, a biocentric perspective is taken, the values held give plants and animals an equal or even higher right to exist. Hence the battle that is going on in the Elaho Valley for the preservation of ancient trees, for not only does intense conflict ensue between those profiting from logging jobs and those demanding a halt to logging, but also the escalation to civil disobedience is quite rapid as environmental depredation, fear for survival, and common fate are equated.

I recall one time as a teenager, sitting around in a warehouse at Ontario Central Airways, sharing a beer and downing the occasional mouthful of caviar from a sturgeon that my friends, a bush pilot and a Cree, had just brought into town. The bush pilot was teasing our aboriginal friend, claiming that "the Indians were tearing down the walls of the houses the government had built for them to keep their fires going." Our Cree friend looked out at the mine headframe on the horizon, at the log boom in the bay, and gently replied, "It must be something we learned from the white man."

Perhaps a biocentric perspective on the environment is inevitable, even for those who believe that the highest value they can place on environmental health is human survival. Only if the elements of the earth, air, and water, renewed by sufficiently great reserves of wilderness, are functioning as they must on their own can human life achieve long-term health and fulfilment. That much we already know.

Notes

1 Oscar Wilde, *A Woman of No Importance*, Act I, in Merlin Holland, ed., *The Oscar Wilde Anthology* (New York: HarperCollins, 2000).
2 Harold Innis, in Daniel Drache, ed. *Staples, Markets and Cultural Change* [Selected Essays of Harold Innis] (Montreal: McGill-Queen's University Press, 1995).
3 Mark Hume, "Fish Flounder in Face of Alcan's Clout," *Vancouver Sun*, January 8, 1991.
4 Premier Mike Harcourt announced the scrapping of Kemano Completion on 23 January 1995.

Works Cited

Tataryn, Lloyd. *Dying for a Living*. Ottawa: Deneau and Greenberg, 1979.
Windsor, James. *Water Export: Should Canada's Water Be for Sale?* Cambridge ON: Canadian Water Resources Research Association, 1992.

13

Romancing Labrador*
The Social Construction of Wilderness and the Labrador Frontier

Peter Armitage

Dear land of mountains, woods and snow, Labrador, our Labrador.
God's noble gift to us below, Labrador, our Labrador. Thy proud
resources waiting still, Their splendid task will soon fulfill,
Obedient to thy Maker's will, Labrador, our Labrador....
—Harry L. Paddon, *Ode to Labrador*, ca. 1927

Cain's land, "Kingdom of Beelzebub," bleak, grim, appalling, and desolate, a tortured land, a primeval, untamed wilderness, rugged and primitive, gaunt and empty, lonely and forlorn, a "Cinderella of the Empire," unmapped and untrodden, frozen frontier, wasteland, land of myriad charms, fathomless beauty, a land barely rippled by time, "Pompeii of the New World," resource Eldorado, storehouse of natural wealth, fisherman's and hunter's paradise, a land of mystery, boundless natural beauty, grandeur, and endless adventure, happy hunting ground, a "Red Man's demesne," Native homeland, Nitassinan, Nunatsiavut. This is Labrador.

---

*The famous medical missionary Sir Wilfred Grenfell (1865–1940) published a book with a similar title in 1934—*The Romance of Laborador*. Arriving in Newfoundland in 1892 as an evangelical missionary with the Royal National Mission to Deep Sea Fishermen, Grenfell played the leading role in establishing medical services in northern Newfoundland and Labrador until his death.

Labrador is, and always has been, an imaginary place, a state of mind, as well as a fact of geography and nature. Our experience of this place over time has been by way of direct contact or through discourses of various types. Basque whalers, New England privateers, Newfoundland fishers, Innu, Inuit, geologists, surveyors, gentleman explorers, missionaries, doctors, botanists, ornithologists, anthropologists, journalists, tourists, traders, administrators, air force personnel, and many others have visited or lived in Labrador over the years. Many of them have had something to say about the place, which has been transmitted to future generations by way of text or oral tradition.

Certainly, discourses about Labrador concern more than its physical characteristics—its climate, vegetation (or lack thereof), topography, geology, fish, game, and abundant insect life. They also concern the human occupants of the territory—the Innu, Inuit, and Settler (Metis) peoples as well as the more recent immigrants from Britain, France, Newfoundland, and mainland Canada.[1] Like most discourses about people and place, the ones about Labrador convey particular ideas that in the social sciences are referred to as "images," "representations," or "constructs," and which harbour "themes," "propositions," or "paradigms."

These mental constructs were built up over time as a result of complex cultural processes that involve the use of pre-existing models of social and natural organization. Old World ideas from our pagan and Judeo-Christian traditions about civilization versus wilderness and the civilized versus the "savage" have supplied some of the foundational materials used to build our perceptions of Labrador and its people, as have various philosophical and artistic currents from the Enlightenment and Romantic periods in European history. Darwinian-inspired notions of human and social evolution, nation-building concerns with frontiers and resource development, and urban-based preoccupations with outdoor recreation and conservation have also provided building blocks.[2]

My aim in this essay is to investigate the imaginary Labrador through its multiple representations in discourse. However, to tackle the entire corpus of Labrador discourse since Jacques Cartier labelled it "the land God gave to Cain" in 1534 is far too ambitious a project. There is clearly enough depth and breath to the Labrador narrative as a whole to warrant book-length consideration. I propose, instead, to conduct a *lecture flotante*, an exploratory tour, an intuitive and interpretative survey, of a small sample of discourses about Labrador that illustrates key themes, propositions, or paradigms about the place.[3]

Today, the student of Labrador affairs must take stock of these key themes, propositions, or paradigms because they provide the cultural lenses through which we view current events there, be they debates over hydro-electric development and military flight training or discussions of public problems, such as gas-sniffing Innu youth and wildlife conservation. At the same time, the student must remember that there are often multiple, competing discourses about Labrador, some of which achieve dominance in the discursive realms in which they are expressed, while others remain muted or marginal at best. For example, until recent times, the voices of Labrador's native people have not been heard in public discourse. And, on occasion, the content of particular discourses has been contested by members of competing ethnic groups within Labrador and among elite groups with interests in the Labrador frontier.

In order to organize our thinking about the multiple discourses about Labrador, I have chosen to categorize them thematically as: (1) Labrador the primeval wilderness; (2) the romantic Labrador; (3) Labrador the resource Eldorado; and (4) native voices from Labrador. In so doing, I recognize that many discourses about Labrador do not fit neatly into these categories; that some of them are replete with ambiguities that shade from one category to the next.

Labrador the Primeval Wilderness

In his sweeping historical analysis of the genesis of the wilderness idea in American culture, Roderick Nash (44) notes that until Romanticism took hold in the late eighteenth and early nineteenth centuries, the dominant view of "wild" places was that they were repulsive, solitary, mysterious, and chaotic. Jacques Cartier's reference to "Cain's land" makes sense in this context, given the hostility toward such "cursed and ungodly" places typical of his time. As for the indigenous inhabitants, they were measured by yardsticks that compared religion, political organization, and technology, and which meant, from the European perspective, that Christians were superior to non-Christians, states to non-states, and iron technologies to stone-based ones (Berkhofer 1978). Places like Labrador, and their peoples, were therefore typecast as the antithesis of agriculture, settlement, and civilization. Nevertheless, the image of Labrador that emerges from early published accounts is much more ambivalent than we might expect.

For the first part of the nineteenth century, the only non-Innu people to penetrate the Labrador interior were employees of the Hudson's Bay

Company, such as John McLean who travelled from Fort Chimo (Kuujjuaq) to North West River–Sheshatshiu in 1839 in search of a good, overland travel route between company posts.[4] Escorted across the Labrador peninsula by Innu guides, McLean was the first European to see the "stupendous" Grand Falls that "exceeds in height the falls of Niagara, but bears no comparison to that sublime object in any other respect" (Wallace 1968). The legend of Grand Falls started here; a legend that inspired many others to venture there in the years to come.[5]

In 1861, Trinity College (Toronto) professor Henry Youle Hind mounted an expedition into the Labrador heartland by way of the Moisie River, which empties into the Gulf of St. Lawrence. According to Hind, "Taken as a whole, it is a region unfit for the permanent abode of civilized man; and although once rich in fur-bearing animals, and in caribou or reindeer, it is now in many parts almost a desert" (1863, 8, vol. 1). Despite this harsh judgment, however, Hind was greatly impressed by the sublime beauty of much of the landscape he traversed: "The pure and invigorating air sighed past us, perceptibly perfumed with the fragrant Labrador tea-plant; and, being all in excellent condition and in the enjoyment of perfect health, we felt glad and thankful that we possessed the rare opportunity of seeing Nature in these silent and distant solitudes" (143). He was also impressed with the country skills of his guides and other Innu he encountered during his trip, and included a great deal of ethnographic detail in his account: "Water in rapid motion is a terrible power, and none know how to take advantage of its humours better than the wild Indian salmon-spearer, who avoids its dangers with matchless skill and self-possession, who is prompt to decide in cases of peril or difficulty, and who seeks the excitement it offers as if it were the main-spring of his life or the aim of his existence" (103).

As the century progressed, new interest in Labrador emerged from various quarters, including the Canadian government and British and American explorers. Interest in the commercial possibilities of resource exploitation in Labrador grew, and some of the first, tentative efforts at mapping and geological exploration were made. By 1890, the American frontier as a meeting place between "savagery" and civilization had been declared closed (Drinnon 1980, 461; Nash 2001, 147), and it would seem that many Americans, particularly those in the New England states, turned their heads toward Labrador as one of the last wild and unexplored areas on the continent.

Writing in 1893, Henry Bryant, of the Geographical Club of Philadelphia, explained "that the great peninsula of Labrador, although probably the first part of the American mainland to be seen by Europeans, contains to-day the largest unexplored area on the Western Continent" (1). Bryant had raced students from the Bowdoin College Scientific Expedition to Labrador to the Grand Falls in 1891, and had become the first person to capture the magnificent cataract in photograph: "A single glance showed that we had before us one of the greatest waterfalls in the world. Standing at the rocky brink of the chasm, a wild and tumultuous scene lay before us, a scene possessing elements of sublimity and with details not to be apprehended in the first moments of wondering contemplation" (30).

A youthful, naive exuberance bubbles from the pages of these early accounts of the first efforts to penetrate the interior and verify reports from Innu and voyageurs of natural wonders such as the Grand Falls. But at the same time, a negative valence continues to punctuate the discourse, continuing well into the twentieth century.

Searching for poetic parallels from other parts of Canada in order to contextualize the Churchill Falls hydroelectric project, Michael Wardell (1967, 20) borrowed from Robert Service in portraying Labrador as "a lost and empty land of forest, lake and river, the land of the bleak, bald-headed North." In 1977, Time-Life published a book by Robert Stewart on Labrador as part of a series on "the world's wild places." In describing Labrador's topography, the author claimed that "Few areas of the earth reflect their tortured evolution so dramatically as does Labrador" (36). Philip Smith, in his history of the Churchill Falls project, described Labrador as "Gaunt and empty, a place of ancient rock and rivers, of lakes and swamps and stunted, tattered trees, it has never been an easy land to live in" (1975, vi). For Davidson and Rugge (1988, 3), "the entire Ungava-Labrador peninsula remains a vast roadless wilderness of mosquito-infested bogs, windswept barrens, and lakes without names." And, in their history of the Iron Ore Company of Canada, Geren and McCullogh (1990, 1) labelled Labrador a "harsh, forbidding place, a vast landscape consisting at various points of fjords, forests, tundra, muskeg, rivers and lakes, especially lakes," while admitting that it is also a "place of haunting beauty."

We read of Labrador as "Canada's desolate corner" in the *National Geographic*, which has served as the Western world's portal to the planet's cultural and geographic nooks and crannies for several decades. "A rough-hewn magnet for Innu Indian caribou hunters, coastal Inuit, Basque whalers, hardy Moravian missionaries, and British fishermen, Labrador has long been a testing ground for human grit" (Poole 1993, 9).

The Romantic Labrador

This notion that Labrador could provide a testing ground for human grit, a territory where one's manhood could be matched against the rigors and perils of the barrens, insect hordes, and wild rivers, is partly what enticed various gentlemen explorers to its lakes, rivers, and shores throughout the twentieth century. The conviction that it was a last frontier where nature could be witnessed in its raw primitiveness and its inhabitants encountered in a state uncorrupted by civilization was also a major driving force behind exploration.[6]

I have already mentioned expeditions to Grand (Churchill) Falls by Henry Bryant and students from Bowdoin College. These had the air of the amateur about them rather than serious scientific endeavors, but they constituted the bedrock for explorations in the first half of the twentieth century by a number of American and British adventurers—Leonidas and Mina Hubbard, Dillon Wallace, William Brooks Cabot, Hesketh Prichard, Herman J. Koehler, Gino Watkins, and Elliott Merrick, to name the most prominent among them. Labrador was made known to many English-speaking members of the Western world through the writings of these people.

In a period of growing dissatisfaction with the constraints of urban life, and a longing for the heroic exploits of earlier explorers and rugged pioneers, Leonidas Hubbard and his two companions, Dillon Wallace and George Elson, set off across Labrador in 1903 only to get lost fifty kilometres from their point of origin at North West River. Jack London's *Call of the Wild* had just been published, and Robert Peary was about to make another attempt on the North Pole (Davidson and Rugge 1988, 4). After weeks of dragging their canoes up the Susan River, chewed by insects and finding little game, Hubbard died of starvation, while Wallace and Elson barely made it back alive. But despite the naivety and apparent incompetence of his venture, there was something heroic in Hubbard's exploits that found great sympathy with the American public. Two years later, his wife, Mina, mounted another expedition to complete her husband's unfinished work, and so that his "name should reap the fruits of service which had cost him so much" (20). This second expedition was conducted in competition with Dillon Wallace, whom she believed had slighted the memory of her husband in his account of the failed expedition, *The Lure of the Labrador Wild.*[7]

Recounting his competitive second trip across Labrador in 1905, Wallace attempted to explain what motivated the gentleman explorer to attempt such exploits:

You who have smelled the camp fire smoke; who have drunk in the pure forest air, laden with the smell of the fir tree; who have dipped your paddle into untamed waters, or climbed mountains, with the knowledge that none but the red man has been there before you; or have perchance, had to fight the wilds and nature for your very existence; you of the wilderness brotherhood can understand how the fever of exploration gets into one's blood and draws one back again to the forests and the barrens in spite of resolutions to "go no more." (1982, 1–2)

The desire to meet the "red man" in his native habitat and the fever of exploration infected others as well. Exploring the barrens west of Nain in 1910, by way of the Fraser River, Hesketh Prichard described the terrain as the "Kingdom of Beelzebub" due to the bloodthirsty swarms of mosquitoes and other tribulations he encountered on his trip. Prichard thought it curious that "such a tract should exist under the British flag, within a comparatively short distance from our shores, and moreover situated actually next door to our oldest colony of Newfoundland" (1911, 1–2). Despite the hardships, however, he found reason to assign some positive attributes to the forgotten land:

It may be asked why any human being should wish to visit such a wilderness as the interior. The answer is that there a man can enjoy the true life of the open, because the land has a charm all its own; perhaps because there is a faint feeling that in some such surroundings our fore-fathers lived out their lives…. As to the scenery of the coast, nothing can well be imagined of its grandeur and impressiveness. (1911, 8)

The Bostonian explorer William Brooks Cabot, who made repeated trips to northern Labrador as a kind of amateur ethnologist, pronounced a similar rationale for his interest in the territory:

Whatever its economic future, the invitation of the country to the wilderness traveler, the traveler with a taste for unworn places, is unusual. Nowhere are such clear, unfished rivers, mapped and unmapped, large rivers and small…. Nor is it easy in this day to find the primitive hunter life as unchanged over a large country as in Labrador. Over their great territory the people still wander at will, knowing no alien restraint, no law but their own. (1920, 5)

In 1929, Elliott Merrick, a young American from New Jersey, was recruited for volunteer work in Labrador with the International Grenfell

Association, where he fell in love with an Australian nurse by the name of Kate Austin.[8] Together, in the fall of 1930, they joined a Settler trapper from North West River by the name of John Michelin on his trap line above the Height of Land on the Labrador plateau. To a major extent, Merrick's love of Labrador and his esteem for its Settler folk was a flight from the mind-dulling anomie of city life, with its "dirt and smell and ugliness," where people work like "stupid ants at a task patently not worth the doing" (1935, 4–5). Ronald Rompkey has described well the "hardy romanticism" of Merrick's writing; the influence of Henry David Thoreau, the traces of Rousseau and the Calvinist idea of salvation through hard work, and his admiration of independence, self-sufficiency, and the "noble savage" (1992, xvi–xxi). In what is one of the greatest works of Labrador literature, *True North*, Merrick shares this introspective moment with the reader:

> Travelling on a track like this is perpetual romance for me. This stump right here, this birch, this snowed-up brook; no, it is not these; it is on and on and forever on through the bright white wilderness and the shadowed trees. And best of all is to stand on a ridge and look ahead over infinities of nameless solitary country dreaming in the short winter sun. And who know the glens and mysteries we may see way off over the hills, and the old Indian camps with buried heaps of rocks that were fireplaces in caribouskin [*sic*] wigwams long before the days of stoves and rifles. Something keeps calling, on and on to the farthest ridges that lean against the sky. And I am convinced that it is not just fancy. It is real and concrete. It is happiness, calling, "Come and take me if you are strong enough." (1935, 181)

Like Prichard, Cabot, Koehler, Grenfell, and others, Merrick shared the view that the Innu people of Labrador were destined to disappear through disease, assimilation, or their own cultural maladaptation. It was an opinion accepted in the nascent social sciences as well, which during this period were busy scurrying about the continent in the shadow of Franz Boaz to record the dying folklore of Native peoples.[9] This commitment to salvage ethnology is what brought Frederick Waugh of the Geological Survey of Canada to northern Labrador in 1920, and American anthropologist William Duncan Strong there as well as part of the second Rawson-MacMillan Subarctic Expedition in 1927–28. In the same period, Franz Boaz's former student Frank Speck was making frequent visits to the Innu on the Quebec North Shore, and was in regular correspondence with Voisey's Bay trader Richard White, from whom he purchased much ethnographic material from the barren ground Innu (Naskapi).

While the driving force for all of these inquiries into Labrador's land and peoples was an infatuation with last frontiers and the last authentic Natives, Labrador was soon presented in a more benign, tamer light that would appeal to the urban tourist. Perhaps the earliest tourism proponent was P.W. Browne. In *Where the Fishers Go*, he wrote, "The trip to Labrador is unique: to the denizen of the grimy city, it bespeaks restful days; to the busy man-of-affairs, it discloses possibilities undreamed of; to the invalid, it brings the balmy breeze of health" (1909, vii). For Browne, Labrador, "the land of the Midnight Sun" and "myriad charms" could be reached easily and inexpensively from New York by steamer via Halifax and St. John's (1909, 331). Two decades later, Sir Wilfred Grenfell concluded that "the chief contribution which Labrador promises to the world in the immediate future is the unique field for tourist traffic" (1934, 326).

With wilderness in increasingly short supply, on a planet suffering from environmental degradation and overpopulation, Labrador continues to hold this appeal, something that the provincial government likes to highlight in its tourism publicity:

> Your wildest dreams. Unique and exotic … this land of boundless beauty and endless adventure. Labrador! There are few places remaining on earth that offer such a rich combination of nature's wonders, fascinating experiences, wilderness adventure, and unique history.… Labrador has the power to unlock your spirit of adventure and awaken your wildest dreams! (Government of Newfoundland and Labrador, Dept. of Tourism, Culture, and Recreation, 2001)

Evidently, this type of tourism marketing invites visitors to blinker themselves from certain Labrador realities, such as the timber-strewn shoreline of Michikamau Lake and other water bodies that comprise the massive Smallwood Reservoir; open-pit iron mines; commercial logging; and thousands of years of aboriginal land use that defy our simplistic notions of pristine wilderness.

The Resource Eldorado

While government tourism brochures and adventure writers continue to celebrate the vastness and natural beauty of Labrador, a vigorous interest in developing its natural resources has existed in parallel with these more romantic discourses for several decades. Sir Wilfred Grenfell and his colleagues did much to stimulate this interest through their efforts to counter the image of Labrador as a backward and destitute hinterland (which Grenfell himself had played a role in shaping through his fundraising efforts in the US and Canada). Grenfell pointed to Labrador's potential for self-sufficiency that could be achieved if its resources were developed. Noting that the "adaptation of Nature, now that man has such marvelous powers over it, is a password to better days," Grenfell spoke of Labrador's fisheries, "which are ever producing their stock of wealth," as well as the "potential of its geologic formation…the same geologic formation as that which has made Canada the richest precious metal producing country in the world" (1934, 325, 328). He concurred with E.M. Kindle, whose research in the Lake Melville area suggested that Labrador would play a very important role "in supplying forest products for the world market of the future" (Grenfell 1934, 326; Kindle 1924, 37).

In bequeathing the anthem "Ode to Labrador" to future generations, Grenfell's Labrador lieutenant, Harry Paddon, transformed this optimism into something teleological. Paddon's lyrics tell us that the territory's natural resources are a gift to the people of Labrador from God, and that their development would be God's will. The forests would soon respond to the lumberjack's axe, and the mighty river floods would be restrained by hydroelectric dams.[10]

On the other hand, as Richard Gwyn reveals, Newfoundland's first premier, Joey Smallwood, thought that Labrador's resources were the "one lucky break that nature gave to Newfoundlanders, a compensation for their climate, isolation, and sparse natural resources. 'It is our chance, perhaps our one chance…to give something back to Canada for all she has given us. It is our chance to stand on our own feet, to do something ourselves. You don't think we like accepting welfare cheques, do you?'" (1968, 240).

In the 1950s, as the Quebec North Shore Railway chugged its way north from Sept-Iles on the Quebec North to Schefferville and Labrador City, many writers saluted exuberantly man's conquest of nature and the transformations wrought by technological progress:

> Labrador is one of the last great unexplored regions of the world and has given evidence of being a vast store-house of economic wealth. Its development has constituted a challenge to the vision and ingenuity of man and the measure of the acceptance of this challenge is to be found in the iron operations in the hinterland, the exploration of the hydro potential of the Hamilton Falls, and other investigations that are now in progress. (Perlin 1959, 118)

Intended as a promotional pamphlet for the recruitment of workers in the new iron ore mines, Ewart Young's *Labrador's Red Gold* talks of "sturdy Newfoundlanders" going north to build an "industrial empire in the wastes of Labrador," which was a "no-man's-land before prospectors and miners pushed back the frontier of civilization to change the face of the north.... Prior to the Iron Ore Company's 'invasion' of the north this territory was visited only by roving bands of Indians." Such was the setting for *The Land God Gave to Cain*, by popular fiction writer Hammond Innes, about a geological survey team in the "savage wastes of Labrador."

In the post-war period, as the economic importance of the cod fishery began to wane and Newfoundlanders sought economic salvation through industrialization, the development of the province's natural resources assumed ever-increasing importance. One writer, John Parsons, held great hopes for the development of Labrador's hydro and forest resources. The forests would "bring the next great boom of industrialization to Labrador, especially so because the demand in Canada for pulp and paper continues to grow each year. There is enough black spruce forest in Labrador to supply several pulp and paper mills" (1970, 160).

In Canada's centennial year, *The Atlantic Advocate* magazine devoted an entire issue to "Newfoundland's contribution to the wealth of Canada by the development of Churchill Falls," with congratulatory letters from Governor General Roland Michener, and Prime Minister Lester B. Pearson.[11] Enunciating the now well-worn cliché that rivers left to run freely to the sea is money lost, Michael Wardell proudly announced that "The roaring masses of water which have thundered down over the giant falls for thousands of years untamed are now about to be harnessed. The mighty potential for power which has wasted itself through the ages in the Labrador wilderness will now be transformed into electrical units ... to serve the needs of modern man over a radius of a thousand miles" (1967, 20). Writing about the "Billion-dollar dream come true," *Reader's Digest* contributor Paul Friggens pointed to the paradox of drying up the "spectacular waterfalls" which are higher than Niagara, but which would "guarantee Canada 5,225,000 kilowatts—seven million cheap horsepower—for industrial and domestic use" (1969, 34). What had once been celebrated as "one of the grandest spectacles of the world" had been reduced to an ignominious trickle.

These texts joined the ranks of two epic accounts about the industrialization of Labrador, told by Geren and McCullogh in the case of the iron ore mines in western Labrador, and Philip Smith in the case of Churchill Falls. They are part of a unique genre of Canadian literature that celebrates the nation-building and heroic efforts of modern-day pioneers who brought civilization and progress to our northern latitudes.[12] Of course, not all Canadians, especially the "reluctant Canadians" who comprise the country's First Nations, have shared the industrial vision found in such texts, especially when the consequences of conquering the north include the alienation of Native homelands and environmental degradation.

Native Voices

In all that has been said about Labrador so far, none of it has flowed from the mouths or pens of people who were actually born there. It is not until the 1970s, in fact, that people native to Labrador, be they Innu, Inuit, Settler (Metis) or landed immigrants, begin to express themselves directly to the outside word. Elizabeth Goudie's *Woman of Labrador*, published in 1973, is one of the first texts that describes the Settler way of life in the early years of the twentieth century from an indigenous perspective. Her son, Horace, contributed his own biography, *Trails to Remember*, in 1991. Both texts present romantic portrayals of the trapper culture of central Labrador, tempered by a stoic acceptance of the hardships that this way of life entailed, and the benefits that came with the construction of a massive air force base in Goose Bay in 1941:

> I enjoy my way of living. Working in the bush is the most wonderful thing in my life, and I plan to go on trapping, hunting and fishing as long as my physical health allows me to.... But there was already a big difference in the lifestyle for most Labradorians because of the Goose Bay air base. Many were lucky enough to get permanent jobs and that was the beginning of a completely new way of life for most trappers. It meant that most of those former trappers who still practice their trade today do it more or less as a hobby. (H. Goudie 1991, 161–62)

Originally from Carbonear, Newfoundland, the charismatic "father" of Charlottetown, Labrador, Benjamin W. Powell, has been a prolific writer of Labrador stories, anecdotes, and personal memoirs. Powell and other family members ran a fish camp and a small, charter aircraft company for many years from their tiny community on the south coast of Labrador. Says Powell:

> Coastal Labrador has many beautiful rivers that empty into the ocean. From Forteau in Labrador south to Nain in Labrador North, we have

approximately twenty rivers. To fly over these rivers by airplane is a
wonderful sight. The rivers wind back and forth, some with their water
going over the high waterfalls. At times, trout and salmon can be seen
leaping high in the air as they slowly go over the waterfall and head for
the spawning areas many miles upstream. (1997, 152)

Them Days magazine, edited for many years by Cartwright native Doris
Saunders, has been a mainstay in the recording of Labrador narratives from
the elder population of the pre-war years, who knew what life without
snowmobiles, electricity, and televisions truly meant. Many outsiders view
Labrador through the pages of this journal, although in the past, it has
had a marked bias toward material concerning the Settler (Metis) and Inuit
peoples.

Whether expressing themselves through texts or songs, Labrador's Eng-
lish-speakers have been more successful in reaching outside audiences than
the Innu and Inuit peoples, whose English-language skills have been limited or non-existent. This linguistic barrier has created a lack of comprehension of Innu and Inuit cultures reminiscent of the great solitudes that divide
the French and the English in Canada. It has only been since the advent of
new aboriginal political organizations in the mid-1970s, and, paradoxically
perhaps, the assimilating effects of formal schooling took hold, that Innu and
Inuit have found an audible voice. Even so, much of what they have to tell
us is mediated by journalists, academics, and other third-party commenta-
tors (e.g., Wadden, Lowe, Pratt, Samson). As far as the Labrador Innu are
concerned, few have yet to explain themselves directly to the outside world,
or within the Innu communities, by way of the written word, unlike the situation in Quebec, where literacy in Innu-aimun is increasingly valued by the
resident Innu.[13] Innu music, on the other hand, is flourishing in Labrador
Innu communities.

Two texts have helped to break the silence of the Labrador Innu as far
as the written word is concerned, both compiled with the assistance of a non-
Innu editor. They are as close as we get, at the moment, to a literature by
and about Labrador Innu. In 1995, Camille Fouillard published the report
of an Innu people's inquiry into a tragic house fire in Davis Inlet that killed
six children. The document presents a comprehensive and honest effort by
the Labrador Innu to consider the causes of their current grief and find
solutions for the future. Frequently, contrasts were drawn, at the time romantic, between the country life in the pre-settlement period and contemporary
existence in the villages. Here is Innu elder Tshishennish Pasteen:

In Davis Inlet today, there are all kinds of problems. It's not like life in
the past. All the people used to respect the animals. Every part of the
animal is important. The skull has to be hung on the tree. At my age
now, I have seen so many caribou bones being thrown away outside the
house. The dogs eat the bones. It really hurts me to see these things
happened. I myself have always respected everything that comes from
the animals. This is how so many bad things happen to us. We can't
blame our problems on alcohol. We have to blame ourselves too, for not
taking care of the caribou bones. (Fouillard, 15)

Innu women's voices were presented more directly to the reading public in the edited collection, *It's Like the Legend* (Byrne and Fouillard 2000).
One finds an honesty in these pages that challenges the tidy, symbolic oppo-
sitions between country-community, white-Innu, and hunting-wage employment found in other texts by non-Innu authors. Here is Caroline Andrew:
"I like to follow some of the ways of the White people, because sometimes
we need them. For example, I am happy to learn their language. It is hard
to find translators when we want to talk to White people, especially when
we see a doctor and important people like the band manager. I get jobs from
White people, because my family needs money to buy things" (131).

In recent years, as Labrador Innu demographics have shifted dramatically in favour of youth, the importance of hunting, trapping, fishing, and living for many months of the year at remote bush camps has decreased. The
Voisey's Bay nickel mine, commercial logging, and new hydroelectric development on the Churchill River are seen by many youth as sources of employment and badly needed income. Innu have come to see themselves as
impoverished, rather than simply a distinctive people, and like many Canadians, want to escape their poverty. This is the context for the talk of former Innu Nation president Peter Penashue to Toronto's Bay Street business
elite:

I firmly believe that the only way to ensure the future of our nations
is to become self-sufficient economically, so we can meet the needs of
our people for housing, education, recreation, and employment without having to depend on Ottawa or anyone else for support. History tells
us that nations able to meet their own needs will become self-govern-
ing and succeed as nations; those that do not or cannot will fail.... I
believe that Innu participation in projects like Voisey's Bay is part of
the solution. Through the agreements we've negotiated with Inco,
many of these same young people now have opportunities to obtain

training and secure, well-paying jobs at the mine. Hope is a powerful thing—and it is turning some of these kids around. (2002, A23)

Among Labrador's Inuit people, a public broadcasting corporation called the OkâlaKatiget Society, located in Nain, has provided Inuttut and English-language programming to Inuit since 1984.[14] Equipped with state-of-the art video and editing equipment, the society prepares television and radio documentaries and feeds to CBC North television as well as community stations. Despite its successes in reaching Inuit audiences, however, OkâlaKatiget lacks the resources to represent Inuit history, culture, issues, and aspirations to the outside world, meaning that representational processes are still heavily mediated by non-Inuit people.

Conclusion

"Romancing Labrador" is evidently my own narrative about Labrador narratives, a discourse about discourses, and one that has been extremely selective in its sampling of the large body of writings about Labrador. It reflects in part my bias towards the territory's interior, an area of primary concern to the Innu people with whom I have been working as an anthropologist for more than two decades. Furthermore, most of the examples presented here point to the social construction of wilderness rather than representations of people and their cultures.

For a population of only thirty thousand people, it is perhaps surprising that the discourses about Labrador are almost as numerous as its insect populations. Labrador is a complicated ethnic mosaic with a complicated history, which explains in part why the discourses about the place are so abundant.

One direction for future research is the multiple ways in which discourses compete with one another and become dominant over time, something I alluded to in the introduction. For example, Rompkey describes an intriguing disagreement in the early 1920s between Sir Wilfred Grenfell and Sir Richard Squires, the prime minister of Newfoundland at the time. Squires was outraged at Grenfell's portrayal of Newfoundland during his lecture circuit in the United States and accused the medical missionary of "'blackmailing' Newfoundland so that he could extract more money for his endowment campaign" (Rompkey 1991, 211). Evidently, news coverage of Grenfell's appeals for financial support contained propositions that the Newfoundland government thought needed to be contested.

Another example is from the 1980s, when Labrador Innu mounted a vigorous opposition to a NATO Tactical Fighter and Weapons Training Centre
proposed for Goose Bay. Innu politicians made public claims about their
traditional hunting culture and how it was being threatened by existing
low-level flying and plans for expansion. In reaction, regional and provincial politicians, and members of competing ethnic groups in Labrador,
attempted to undermine the symbolic resources used by the Innu when
making such claims by likening their land use to the "rich sportsman's idea
of a vacation," underlining their dependence on government funding, and
citing examples of lack of respect for the environment (Armitage and
Kennedy 1989).

In the end, no systematic analysis of Labrador discourses will be complete without research into the conditions underlying the production of the
discourses in the first place. As Michel Foucault has noted, "the production
of discourse is at once controlled, selected, organized and redistributed
according to a certain number of procedures" (1971, 8). The task at hand,
then, is to analyze the cultural and political contexts in which discourse is
produced, as well as the strategies and tactics employed to control, select,
organize, and distribute discourses about that great land called Labrador
and its peoples.

The need to understand how power is exercised in shaping public discourses about places like Labrador makes sense to those who want to know
the grammar of public problems and environmental debates over issues
such as hydroelectric development, commercial forestry, mining, the establishment of parks, or military flight training. Moreover, the need to understand the thinking of rural and northern peoples and the opinion leaders who
shape public policy about such places is fundamental. The premise for all
of this is that public opinion is never a tabula rasa when it comes to undertaking advocacy work related to northern issues. The slate has been well
marked by decades, if not hundreds of years, of ideas and images that are
transported intergenerationally by way of discourse. Neophytes to northern
politics who ignore the history of discourses about northern places and
their influence over contemporary political life do so at their peril.

Notes

1 Until the 1980s, the majority of people in Labrador who claimed mixed European and Inuit ancestry used terms like "Settler" and "Native Labradorians" to
   describe themselves. Today, most call themselves "Inuit," "Metis," or "Labradorians," and belong either to the Labrador Inuit Association or the Labrador Metis
   Nation. Note that in Labrador, Metis is spelled without "é."

2   I write this as an urban, male, white, Anglo-Saxon Protestant, recognizing that the Canadian multicultural mosaic includes people from other traditions as well as the Judeo-Christian one.

3   See Kirsch and Bernier (1988, 35–47) for more information on this approach to discourse analysis.

4   Captain George Cartwright, who established a trading operation in the Sandwich Bay area of southern Labrador in the last quarter of the eighteenth century, published a *Journal of Transactions and Events, During a Residence of Nearly Sixteen Years on the Coast of Labrador; Containing Many Interesting Particulars, Both of the Country and Its Inhabitants, Not Hitherto Known*, in 1792 (Townsend, 1911). With the exception of a lengthy and romantic "Poetical Epistle" at the back of the journal, there is no eloquence in Cartwright's descriptions of Labrador and the Innu and Inuit people he meets. His accounts of the latter show a marked preference for Inuit demeanour and ambivalence toward the "Mountaineers" (Innu) at best. While admiring the hunting abilities of the Innu, he complains about a perceived propensity for drunkenness and thieving.

5   Renamed "Churchill Falls" by then Premier Joey Smallwood in 1965 in honour of Sir Winston Churchill.

6   See Carolyn Merchant's discussion about the role of a reinvented, Edenic, feminized wilderness in the American recovery narrative. "Nature, wilderness, and civilization are socially constructed concepts that change over time and serve as stage settings in the progressive narrative…. Environmentalism, like feminism, reverses the plot of the recovery narrative, seeing history as a slow decline, not a progressive movement that has made the desert blossom as the rose. The recovery story is false; an original garden has become a degraded desert" (1995, 153, 155).

7   Hubbard's and Wallace's publications from their travels across Labrador have nourished generations of readers, both young and old, in the United States, Canada, and other parts of the world. *The Lure of the Labrador Wild* was assigned reading in the Newfoundland school system for many years.

8   Led by Sir Wilfred Grenfell, the International Grenfell Association was established in 1914.

9   Franz Boaz, the founder of modern American anthropology.

10 Dr. Harry L. Paddon composed the lyrics sometime around 1927. They are sung to the tune of *O Tannebaum* < http://nfldsongs.tripod.com/05/labrador.htm >.

11 The editor's introduction includes a poem, "Flame of Our Future," which reads in part, "From clay to kiln, by pioneers, this land / Was shaped, reshaped and moulded to time's wheel; / Tempered in heat of conquest, through blood-flow…. / Polished in progress, prove the mindful men / Who gathered in the name of nationhood" (p. 17).

12 See also MacLennan's, "The Hamilton: Miracle in Labrador" (1974, 223–36). Examples from Quebec include Réthi and Jacobus (1971), Bourassa (1985), Lacasse (1983), and Turgeon (1992).

13 See An Antane Kapesh's *Eukuan nin matshimanitu Innu-iskueu* (I am a god damn Innu woman), published in Innu-aimun and French, and Desneiges Mollen's *Ushinamutau* (laughing together), a collection of twenty-four amusing stories

that the author heard over the years, written entirely in Innu-aimun. Dr. Marguerite MacKenzie, at Memorial University's Department of Linguistics, printed a short text in Innu-aimun by Sheshatshiu Innu elder Pien Penashue, and Natuashish resident George Rich had one of his texts printed by an adult literacy program he participated in while living in St. John's several years ago. Neither of these documents, however, benefited from the marketing and public distribution normally provided by commercial publishing houses.

14 Labrador Inuit use "Inuttut" rather than "Inuktitut" to designate their language.

Works Cited

Armitage, Peter, and John C. Kennedy. "Redbaiting and Racism on Our Frontier: Military Expansion in Labrador and Quebec." *The Canadian Review of Sociology and Anthropology* 26, 5 (1989): 798–817.

Berkhofer, Robert F. *The White Man's Indian: Images of the American Indian from Columbus to the Present*. New York: Alfred A. Knopf, 1978.

Bourassa, Robert. *Power from the North*. Scarborough: Prentice-Hall Canada, 1985.

Browne, P.W. *Where the Fishers Go: The Story of Labrador*. New York: Cochrane, 1909.

Bryant, Henry G. *A Journey to the Grand Falls of Labrador*. Philadelphia: Geographical Club of Philadelphia, 1893.

Byrne, Nympha, and Camille Fouillard. *It's Like the Legend: Innu Women's Voices*. Charlottetown, PEI: Gynergy Books, 2000.

Cabot, William Brooks. *Labrador*. Boston: Small, Maynard, 1920.

Davidson, James, and John Rugge. *Great Heart: The History of a Labrador Adventure*. New York: Viking, 1988.

Drinnon. R. *Facing West: The Metaphysics of Indian-Hating and Empire Building*. Minneapolis: University of Minnesota Press, 1980.

Foucault, Michel. "Orders of Discourse." *Social Science Information* 10, 2 (1971): 7–30.

Fouillard, Camille. *Gathering Voices: Finding Strength to Help Our Children*. Toronto: Douglas & McIntyre, 1995.

Friggens, Paul. "Churchill Falls: Billion-Dollar Dream Come True." *Reader's Digest* (December 1969): 32–38.

Geren, Richard, and Blake McCullogh. *Cain's Legacy: The Building of Iron Ore Company of Canada*. Sept-Iles: Iron Ore Company of Canada, 1990.

Goudie, Elizabeth. *Woman of Labrador*. Toronto: Peter Martin Associates, 1973.

Goudie, Horace. *Trails to Remember*. St. John's: Jesperson Press, 1991.

Grenfell, Wilfred. *The Romance of Labrador*. New York: Macmillan, 1934.

Gwyn, Richard. *Smallwood: The Unlikely Revolutionary*. Toronto: McClelland & Stewart, 1968.

Hind, Henry Youle. *Explorations in the Labrador Peninsula the Country of the Montagnais and Nasquapee Indians*. London: Longman, Green, Longman, Roberts & Green, 1863, vols. 1–2.

Hubbard, Mina. *A Woman's Way through Unknown Labrador.* St. John's: Breakwater Books, 1981[1908].

Innes, Hammond. *The Land God Gave to Cain.* New York: Alfred A. Knopf, 1958.

Kapesh, An Antane. *Eukuan nin matshimanitu Innu-iskueu.* Sept-Iles: ICEM, 2003
[1979].

Kindle, E.M. *Geography and Geology of Lake Melville District, Labrador Peninsula.*
Geological Survey, Department of Mines, Canada. Ottawa: F.A. Acland, 1924.

Kirsch, Chantal, and Bernard Bernier. "Le sens du discours écrit: propos
méthodologiques à partir de deux recherches." *Culture* 8, 1(1988): 35–47.

Lacasse, Roger. 1983. *Baie James: Une épopée.* Montreal: Libre Expression, 1983.

Lowe, Mick. *Premature Bonanza: Standoff at Voisey's Bay.* Toronto: Between the
Lines, 1998.

MacLennan, Hugh. *Rivers of Canada.* Toronto: Macmillan, 1974.

Merchant, Carolyn. "Reinventing Eden: Western Culture as a Recovery Narrative." In *Uncommon Ground: Toward Reinventing Nature,* ed. William Cronon.
New York: W.W. Norton, 1995. 132–59.

Merrick, Elliott. *True North.* New York: Charles Scribner's Sons, 1935.

Mollen, Desneiges. *Ushinamutau.* Sept-Isles: ICEM, 2004.

Nash, Roderick Frazier. *Wilderness and the American Mind.* New Haven: Yale University Press, 2001[1967].

Parsons, John. *Labrador: Land of the North.* New York: Vantage Press, 1970.

Penashue, Peter. "Why I made peace with Bay Street." *Globe and Mail,* December 3, 2002.

Perlin, A.B. *The Story of Newfoundland.* St. John's: Guardian, 1959.

Poole, Robert M. "Labrador: Canada's Place Apart." *National Geographic* 184,
4(1993): 2–35.

Powell, Benjamin W. *Sport Fishing in Labrador.* St. John's: Good Tidings Press,
1997.

Pratt, Alexandra. *Lost Lands, Forgotten Stories: A Woman's Journey to the Heart of
Labrador.* Toronto: Harper Flamingo, 2002.

Prichard, H. Hesketh. *Through Trackless Labrador.* London: William Heinemann,
1911.

Réthi, Lili, and William W. Jacobus. *Manic 5: The Building of the Daniel Johnson
Dam.* New York: Doubleday, 1971.

Rompkey, Ronald. *Grenfell of Labrador: A Biography.* Toronto: University of Toronto
Press, 1991.

Rompkey, Ronald. Introduction to Elliott Merrick, *The Long Crossing and Other
Labrador Stories.* Orono, MA: University of Maine Press, 1992.

Samson, Colin. *A Way of Life That Does Not Exist: Canada and the Extinguishment
of the Innu.* St. John's: ISER, 2003.

Smith, Philip. *Brinco: The Story of Churchill Falls.* Toronto: McClelland & Stewart, 1975.

Stewart, Robert. *Labrador.* New York: Time-Life, 1977.

Townsend, Charles Wendell, ed. *Captain Cartwright and His Labrador Journal.* Boston: Dana Estes, 1911.

Turgeon, Pierre. *La Radissonie: Le pays de la baie James.* Montreal: Libre Expression, 1992.

Wadden, Marie. *Nitassinan: The Innu Struggle to Reclaim Their Homeland.* Toronto: Douglas & McIntyre, 1991.

Wallace, Dillon. *The Lure of the Labrador Wild.* St. John's: Breakwater Books, 1982[1905].

Wallace, Dillon. *The Long Labrador Trail.* New York: Outing Publishing, 1907.

Wallace, W.S., ed. *John McLean's Notes of a Twenty-Five Years' Service in the Hudson's Bay Territory* (2 vols. London 1849, reprinted by The Champlain Society, Toronto, 1932). Westport, CT: Greenwood, 1968.

Wardell, Michael. "The Thunder of His Power—Who Can Understand?" *The Atlantic Advocate,* July 1967, 20–27.

Young, Ewart. *Labrador's Red Gold.* Labrador Mining and Exploration Company and Iron Ore Company. St. John's: Guardian, ca. 1958.

14

Prey

Jarmo Jalava

I

It wasn't easy to decide how best to exploit three months of parental leave. Should we change twenty diapers a day at a seaside cottage in Newfoundland? Be sleepless on the Queen Charlotte Islands? Pump breast milk in the Falklands? It was clear we wanted big wind, big sky, and big water. And a sense of solitude. One summer afternoon we realized we didn't need to burn quite so much hydrocarbon. It was but a couple of hours by car to a landscape of billion-year-old rock, scoured and sculpted by water and ice, a coast as stunning and elemental as any I have seen.

II

I awake to gunfire. Someone is shooting at something on Franklin Island, the new provincial conservation reserve across the channel. Alison and our newborn son, Noah, are still asleep beside me. We are renting an old plywood cabin that stands in the wind on barren, flesh-toned granite on Georgian Bay, north of Parry Sound. We arrived yesterday and will stay a month, until Thanksgiving. Then we will go to another cottage, on the Lake Huron shore of the Bruce Peninsula, until the end of November.

III

People know me as a biologist, as someone who goes out to the natural world and attaches names to things, living things. I hunt for rare plants and animals, gather data. When I was younger, I did this for fun. I was a naturalist, a birder. That's how I ended up in this job. Now, as a government ecologist, I use such information to help determine which places deserve to be left untouched. It's part of my job to map lines that define where the wild has the credentials to remain wild.

In North America and throughout the world, scientific information is now used to prioritize natural areas for protection. In the past, it was enough that a place possessed some unique or spectacular beauty—that is how many of the first national parks were identified. Today, it is more likely that an area will be preserved if it is the last stronghold of an endangered species. The more rare plants and animals at a site, the better, so we biologists look extra hard for them during our field surveys. On the other hand, most of the world's pristine landscapes are simply "wastelands"—tundra, desert, remote mountain ranges, impenetrable swamps—deemed unworthy for human use.

IV

It's later the same morning, the gunfire has subsided, and I'm sitting on a smooth boulder on the shore. A warm September wind licks my skin, caresses the rocks, kisses the junipers and pines. A lone kayak slices through glistening water in the channel. Horned larks and pipits migrate overhead, using this coastline as a landmark on their journey from the Arctic. Dragonflies fly in coitus from the water to the sky. Gulls glide effortlessly on the breeze. A pileated woodpecker cackles in the forest.

A distant boom mystifies me. Is there a quarry to the north of here? Is someone building a new road? The human conquest continues, incrementally, inevitably, obliviously, somewhere beyond my range of vision, all over the rest of the world.

V

It's our first walk down the one-lane track behind the cottage. Noah is strapped to my breast in a front-carrier. A snowshoe hare darts across the road. From the junipers in pursuit leaps a fisher. The big weasel freezes, assesses us, then slinks back into the shrubs. It re-emerges a moment later, takes a few cautious steps towards the hare, peers at us with suspicious black eyes, and retreats again to the junipers. Alison says she's never seen a fisher before. Unaware that this was something he may never witness, Noah farts.

VI

The next day, the three of us set off for another walk and discover a heap of scat on a patch of bare bedrock in a mossy roadside glade. I say I'm sure it's bear shit, for it's black and laced with berry skins. Minutes later, we encounter the animal, probably just a yearling, not much larger than a New-foundland dog. It lopes lazily along the track ahead, catches our scent, and jerks off the road, trouncing noisily through the woods. It has wisely learned to fear us.

VII

Over the next few days, we watch the waterfowl population grow in the bay next to the cottage. By the end of the week, migrant mallards have arrived to consume submerged aquatic plants. Loons, cormorants, and mergansers dine on minnows. And several scaup ducks dive to the lake bottom to eat the zebra mussels that have invaded Ontario's waters in recent years. The mussels, it is believed, hitchhiked here from the Caspian Sea in the ballasts of ocean freighters. Although these filter-feeders have restored astonishing clarity to murky, polluted waters, their population explosion has, in less than a decade, impaired the Great Lakes ecosystem. Native mussel species have declined, as have fish such as perch that thrive in the naturally cloudy waters of the shallow bays. Washed-up mussel shells tinkle in the surf and gash the soles of barefoot swimmers.

VIII

One evening, I set off in the canoe. There is no wind. The sun has just set. A half-moon shines in the east, and my profession is, for the moment, a faint memory. The dusk sky is ten colours I know and a thousand for which I have no words. Inexpressible combinations of whites, yellows, blues, and grays grade upward from the western horizon. I think of the noise of words. I think of the space between thoughts, the quiet place where Noah lives, where animals dwell, where meditators go. From the forest rises the crazy beauty of a whippoorwill's chant.

Ahead are four silhouettes—the scaup ducks I saw earlier in the day. As I approach, they swim nervously to the right, in the exact trajectory I intend to take. They must think I am chasing them, for they splash across the calm water in a panic. Eventually their tangent angles beyond my arc and they relax. I carry on, thinking how hopeless those ducks' chances would be if I had a shotgun and reasonable aim. Scaup make good eating, or so I hear. If they were wise, they'd have flown. Or maybe they sensed something about me.

I think of the Waorani hunter in the Amazon who can blow-gun dinner from the jungle canopy with a poison dart. I think of Inuit dining on walrus. I think of the argument that humans evolved to hunt, that the hunt connects us with our primordial spirit. I think of the Jain people of western India, who make every effort not to kill a living being, not even a plant or micro-organism.

I paddle on, trying to be perfectly silent, trying to emulate otter, loon, and aboriginal canoe. Summer is over, so gone are the powerboats and Jet Skis that scribble ephemeral signatures as they roar across the water. When winter comes, buzzing snowmobiles will leave slightly more permanent marks as they race across the ice.

The canoe scrapes the sandy bottom of the bay. I realize how far I have strayed. I take a few deep breaths and aim for the light of the cottage. I perceive a background noise, a subliminal hiss. A metropolis of crickets proclaims something huge and inexpressible from cracks in the bedrock. I thank nameless gods.

IX

It's a brisk day, the last of September. I am lying down, on my back, watching small kettles of hawks soar southward. They are miniscule specks, difficult to identify. My concentration is punctuated by random gunshots, three or four at a time. I imagine the testosterone buzz that holding a gun imparts. I understand that hunting can be an art. The emotion of the chase probably bears some resemblance to what our hunting ancestors must have felt. And I can't help but be impressed by the human ingenuity that developed the laser eyepieces hunters use to measure distance to a target animal. But technology seems to blur the distinction between the primal urge and the fetish that compels people to play computer games. These lands and waters are now a playground for guns. Men ride around in all-terrain vehicles, equipped with military gun-mounts, playing war games with other species. Their vehicles leave deep ruts in the soil, ruts that take decades to vanish into the wild anonymity of evolution.

Most of the machines that rumble through these forests, speed across these lakes, and spray pellets at the birds I adore, would break noise bylaws in suburbs. We won't stand for a crying baby in the hush of a movie theatre but we will tolerate gunshots in provincial parks. Our taxes pay for crossing guards on city streets but I must dress my child in "hunter's orange" to walk country trails in the fall.

A flock of four ring-necked ducks flies over the point, toward the gunfire. What's the bag limit for ring-necks, I wonder. The government department that employs me issues the hunting licenses and sets the daily limits for killing and possession of game. In one autumn day, a hunter may legally shoot a deer, ten squirrels, six snowshoe hares, and an unlimited number of woodcocks, Canada geese, skunks, weasels, raccoons, foxes, coyotes, and wolves, and pile them in the back of his pick-up truck to be eaten or stuffed. I've had enough, get up, enter the cabin, and make grilled cheese sandwiches for Alison and me. We watch Noah sleeping peacefully in his little bouncy-chair.

X

The three of us set off for our daily walk. It is brisk and sunny, and ice has formed on the puddles of yesterday's rain. Flocks of blue jays migrate low over the trees. Phoebes, thrushes, and white-crowned sparrows have arrived overnight, navigating by the stars and perhaps with a sixth sense that aligns them with the magnetic field of the earth. They also call to each other. You can hear them on calm nights in spring and fall, if you listen.

Near the end of the long driveway of the cottage lot, we encounter a regal-looking ruffed grouse strutting fearlessly, perhaps stupidly, across the track. A few minutes down the public road we meet a man in a camouflage suit and thick glasses. He is carrying a rifle, with the barrel pointed safely skyward. "Beautiful day, isn't it?" he smiles. We agree. "There's a big old bear, a male, down the road a ways, just past the fork," he adds cheerfully. We thank him for the news.

For the rest of our walk, our senses are heightened in anticipation of seeing the great bear. Alison and I talk about the complexities of the issue of hunting: how ingrained it is in the rural culture, how the abundance of Ontario's wildlife is advertised south of the border, with thousands of people travelling north each autumn to spend American dollars at hunting camps in remote northern communities.

The man we just encountered radiated warmth, and it seemed he was trying to be a good ambassador for the sport, to go out of his way not to intimidate us. I tell Alison that I had wanted to ask the hunter what he was planning to kill today, but that politeness prevented me. We talk about the absence of rites of passage for our youth, about the commodification of nature. Alison asks me what I think a good rite of passage would be. I suggest six months of wilderness solitude, but not during hunting season.

We reach the fork in the road and wait, hoping to see the bear. Pines and scraggly oaks sway in the breeze. Hungry warblers and kinglets glean insects in the branches. We give the bear a few minutes to appear. Then we turn around and are startled by a loud gunshot. I say to Alison that my blond head could easily be mistaken for the behind of a white-tailed deer. Noah is wearing red. I joke that I should hold him up over my head as a safety precaution.

Alison asks me if hunters are permitted to enter private property. I say yes, if the property isn't posted with prohibitive signs. Alison proposes that we make a "No Hunting" sign and hammer it to a tree at the entrance to the cottage driveway. I suggest that this probably isn't necessary, since I think the hunters stay on the Crown Land on the other side of the road.

Alison muses aloud about how lands can be "owned" by humans, how entrenched this ideology is. Abstraction is the human animal's greatest power and its greatest crutch. The globe is a spider web of imaginary borders. Lands seem like solid, fixed entities, so it's possible to mark boundaries, to erect fences, to post "No Trespassing" signs. Barbed wire is stretched between landscapes of divergent human beliefs.

We enter "our" driveway. A few dozen metres in, we encounter the man in camouflage again. "Grouse for dinner tonight," he shouts with pride. I salivate, imagining the roasted bird. I believe in the ecological economy of local food. At the same time, I feel violated. The hunter is plucking feathers. As we walk past I say, with a hint of self-righteousness, that just moments ago we'd admired that very grouse with our binoculars. He calls to our backs, "I'll be admiring it on a bed of rice tonight, with butter-fried mushrooms on the side." We look back with long faces and keep walking.

A few strides further, I meekly add, "This is private property, you know." I don't know if he hears. Although nobody owns the air, I guess it's possible to own what flies.

XI

Two months have passed. We are now staying at the other cottage, the one on the Bruce Peninsula, near Oliphant. Late on a mild November afternoon, I feel I need some time alone. I walk toward the end of a dirt track that leads out to the Lake Huron shore. This is where off-road vehicles access the duck blinds in the marshes. The lake is at its lowest level in thirty years, so you can drive or walk for miles on sandflats that would normally be under a half metre of water.

I sidestep the dismembered limb and decapitated head of a doe that someone left to rot in the grassy median of the drive. Yesterday was the first day of the local deer hunt, and the duck hunt is in full swing. I walk out onto the flats and hear someone blowing a whistle in threes. A man in an orange jacket is standing in the cattails a few hundred metres away, waving his arms. Is he blowing the whistle at me? Or is he signaling to other hunters of my presence? I keep walking, ignoring him. Nobody owns these sands.

The setting sun is a cool clementine. Fifteen pectoral sandpipers are busily probing for invertebrates at the water's edge. I avoid stepping in the puddles that adorn the flats like sparkling jewels of reflected sky. The south wind waltzes with the great lake, and with each step I join the dance, my body light, ethereal. Twelve female buffleheads fly over, silhouetted black against the sun. I hear four gunshots and wonder, oddly unafraid, if I am in the line of fire.

A merlin falcon speeds across the bay and two sanderlings on the far shore crouch in fear. I gaze across the expanse of slate water at a boarded-up cabin. The phrase "you die alone" rings in my head. These wet sands are so vast and flat I feel both huge and small against the horizon.

I walk on. A juvenile plover, so much smaller than me, skitters across the flats. I follow it, trying to scare it up, to hear it call, to see its wing pattern so that I can identify it to species, give it a scientific name. But it won't fly. It just runs and runs and runs. Tundra-born, it has probably never seen a human being before. I let it run.

The sun has dropped below the horizon. I turn around, aim myself toward loved ones, toward home. My eyes trace the truck ruts all over the sand. It won't be long before the winds and rains wash them away.

Three more gunshots. I stop, look up at the sky. So many colours, name-less colours. I look back at my path, bootprints next to plover tracks. Another warm gust of wind and I am a bird. A huge gratitude swells up inside me. Every breath of air is shared. I have tasted my prey.

Contributors

Peter Armitage has worked among aboriginal people in Labrador and northern Quebec as a graduate student, researcher, and consultant for over twenty years. His research has included land use, environmental impacts of resource development and military training activities, ethnicity, and religious belief. He is currently curating museum exhibits for the Provincial Museum of Newfoundland and Labrador, the Innu Nation, and the Canadian Heritage Network, and he assists the Innu Nation with land claims.

Ehor Boyanowsky is a social psychologist who teaches in the School of Criminology at Simon Fraser University (SFU) in Vancouver. His areas of interest include human violence and aggression, and crimes against the environment, an area in which he has pioneered courses. He is a member of the Institute of Fisheries Analysis at SFU, a member of the Board of Directors of the Wild Salmon Center of Portland, Oregon, and of the Habitat Restoration Corporation, and a past president of the Steelhead Society of British Columbia.

Anne Marie Dalton is an associate professor in the Religious Studies Department at St. Mary's University in Halifax. She lectures, researches, and writes in the area of religion and ecology. She is the author of *A Theology for the Earth: The Contributions of Thomas Berry and Bernard Lonergan.*

Trish Glazebrook is an associate professor of philosophy at Dalhousie University. She is the author of *Heidegger's Philosophy of Science*, the editor of a forthcoming collection of essays on Heidegger's critique of science, and is currently finishing a manuscript titled "Eco-Logic: Erotics of Nature." She is a member of the Board of Directors of the International Association of Environmental Philosophers.

Monte Hummel is president of the World Wildlife Fund of Canada. He is the author of *Arctic Wildlife* and *Wintergreen: Reflections from Loon Lake*, co-

author of *Wild Hunters: Predators in Peril*, and the general editor of *Endangered Spaces* and *Protecting Canada's Endangered Spaces*.

Jarmo Jalava is a writer, songwriter, and ecologist residing on Manitoulin Island,
Ontario, and in Tepoztlan, Mexico. He has published more than fifty stories,
poems, magazine and newspaper articles, and ecological reports. He is past
editor of the literary journal *Exile*. After eleven years with the Ontario Min-
istry of Natural Resources, he now works as a consulting ecologist for various conservation-oriented projects. His debut music CD, *Hole in the Sky*,
appeared in 2001.

Karen Krug is an associate professor in the Centre for the Environment at
Brock University in St. Catharines, Ontario. She teaches courses on sustainable agriculture, gender and the environment, human services planning, and environmental ethics. Currently she is principal researcher in a
SSHRC-funded study aimed at identifying ways to build more sustainable
rural-urban agriculture. She and her family are beginning to implement
sustainable urban agriculture at home through permaculture approaches.

Elizabeth May is an environmentalist, writer, activist, lawyer, and executive
director of the Sierra Club of Canada. From 1986-88 she was senior policy
advisor to the federal environment minister. She was a founding member
of the Canadian Environmental Defence Fund and Women for a Healthy
Planet. Her books include *Budworm Battles, Paradise Won: The Struggle to Save
South Moresby, At the Cutting Edge: The Crisis in Canada's Forests*, and (co-
authored with Maude Barlow) *Frederick Street: Life and Death on Canada's Love
Canal*.

Catriona (Cate) Mortimer-Sandilands is an associate professor in the Faculty of Enviromental Studies at York University in Toronto, where she
teaches in the ecotone amid environmental thought, political theory, and
studies of gender and sexuality. Her book *The Good-Natured Feminist: Ecofeminism and the Quest for Democracy* treats questions of identity, voice, and
power in feminist ecological theories and politics. Her current work connects
queer theory and environmental practice, and delves into questions of
national identity and nature in the ongoing development of Canada's
national park system.

Onno Oerlemans taught at the University of Ottawa, and is an associate professor at Hamilton College in Clinton, New York, where he teaches courses
on British Romanticism and literature and the environment. He is the
author of *Romanticism and the Materiality of Nature*.

Lionel Rubinoff is professor emeritus of philosophy and environmental studies at Trent University in Peterborough, Ontario. He also taught at the University of Toronto and York University. He is the author of several books, including *The Pornography of Power* and *Objectivity, Method and Point of View* (with Jan Van Der Dussen). He is completing a book "The Moral Foundations of Environmentalism," as well as editing another book "Science, Moral Accountability, and The New Biology."

Leanne Simpson, born to an Anishinaabeg mother and Scottish father, is a researcher, writer, and advocate for the rights of Indigenous Peoples, and director of the Indigenous Environmental Knowledge Program at Trent University. She was a member of several delegations to the United Nations regarding Traditional Knowledge and the Convention on Biological Diversity, and the trans-boundary regulation of genetically modified organisms. She is an active board member of the Boreal Forest Network and Call of the Earth, an international Indigenous People's Initiative on intellectual property policy.

J.A. Wainwright is a professor of English literature at Dalhousie University in Halifax. He has written a biography of the Canadian writer Charles Bruce and edited a collection of Margaret Laurence's letters to Canadian writers, *A Very Large Soul*. He is also is the author of five books of poetry and two novels, *A Deathful Ridge: A Novel of Everest and A Far Time*.